The Healing Christ

By Robert Winterhalter

PO Box 754, Huntsville, AR 72740
800-935-0045 479-738-2348
www.ozarkmt.com

© 2010 by Robert Winterhalter

Scripture quotations are from the Revised Standard Version of the Bible©
1946, 1952 and 1971 by the Division of Christian Education of the National
Council of Churches of Christ in the USA. Used by permission. All rights
reserved.

All rights reserved. No part of this book, in part or in whole, may be
reproduced, transmitted or utilized in any form or by any means, electronic,
photographic or mechanical, including photocopying, recording, or by any
information storage and retrieval system without permission in writing from
Ozark Mountain Publishing, Inc. except for brief quotations embodied in
literary articles and reviews.

For permission, serialization, condensation, adaptions, or for our catalog of
other publications, write to Ozark Mountain Publishing, Inc., P.O. box 754,
Huntsville, AR 72740, ATTN: Permissions Department.

Library of Congress Cataloging-in-Publication Data
Winterhalter, Robert, 1936-2010
    The Healing Christ, by Robert Winterhalter
Showing the Metaphysical explanations for the healings of Christ that are
mentioned in the Bible.

1. Jesus   2. Healings   3. Bible   4. Metaphysics
I. Winterhalter, Robert, 1936-2010   II. Bible   III. Jesus   IV. Title

Library of Congress Catalog Card Number: 2010922434
ISBN: 978-1-886940-69-7

Cover Art and Layout: www.enki3d.com
Book set in: Times New Roman
Book Design: Julia Degan

Published by:

OZARK
MOUNTAIN
PUBLISHING
PO Box 754
Huntsville, AR 72740

WWW.OZARKMT.COM
Printed in the United States of America

This book is dedicated to Divine Science founder, Malinda E. Cramer.

TABLE OF CONTENTS

Introduction

I represent the movement known as New Thought. This book is written out of over 48 years of experience in the field, as well as that of many colleagues and generations of earlier teachers and healers dating back to the 19th Century. It correlates these generations of experience with the healing work of Jesus of Nazareth, whom we regard as the founder of our science and its greatest practitioner. In the Third Millennium, there is need of a written guide which outlines how the healing records in the Gospels are relevant to our times.

The pattern of Jesus' healing work is apparent to those who are involved, for an extended period, in similar activity today. In this book, I will also bring in many facets of what serious scholarship can say about the Gospel healing records and the languages and cultures of an earlier time. Not every detail in these brief biblical records is accurate, but the authenticity of the basic pattern is clear. This becomes apparent by drawing analogies between current experiences and those of First Century people.

The inadequacies of English translation must, in many cases, be challenged to make things clear for the modern reader.

Unlike Christian Science, the various branches of New Thought will work with students and patients who are also seeking the help of medical doctors, chiropractors, or other branches of the healing arts *at the same time*. Many chiropractors, who relate their understanding of Innate to the indwelling Presence of God, find New Thought teachings to be congenial. Also, recent statements by many medical doctors that there is such a thing as effective prayer has attracted the interest of many of us. Larry Dossey's book, *Prayer is Good Medicine*, is one of many examples. As the dust jacket of *Prayer is Good Medicine* declares, in part: "Based on his groundbreaking work linking prayer and health, physician Larry Dossey offers new ways of working with prayer –and tells us how we can harness its remarkable healing powers."

The Healing Christ refers not to Jesus alone, but to the Christ Identity which is the core of our own being, and that of the cosmos. Jesus was the rabbi from Nazareth. Christ is God's perfect idea of humanity, encompassing both genders equally. Jesus sought to awaken us all to our identity in Christ, to our essential oneness with (to use the term preferred by Dossey) the Absolute.

To achieve rapport with Jesus' ministry as recorded in Matthew, Mark, Luke, and John, it is vital to take Divine healing seriously as a current potential. Old, outworn, mechanical concepts of the universe, or even observations about the power of suggestion, cannot account for the range of healing events found in the Gospel records. More recent insights, such as those in quantum physics, reveal a cosmos in which reality is non-local and material limitations need not exist. In short, time and space are not the absolutes that people once believed them to be.

James Eden, M.D., writing from the background of the modern medical field, has authored a landmark work, *Energetic Healing*. He has a greater openness to what is possible and available than is the case with many of today's religious professionals. It is an anomaly when medical doctors find it necessary to instruct clergy about the power of faith, but such are the times in which we are living. Writing of the society of the future, Eden envisions that people "would be able to see behind the curtain of materialistic illusion, in a personal and collective sense, and would see that the matters of the Spirit take precedence over matters of the material."1

We need to open our minds to the healing effects of "distant prayer" already documented by scientific experiments. We understand that God belongs to everyone, and everyone belongs to God. This is the nature of Omnipresence, which transcends the seeming limitations of time and place.

In several ways, the findings of Dr. Dossey agree with our own experience. For one thing, love, empathy, and deep caring set the stage for successful healing work. Love, which is helpful and effective, however, is inspired by God who *is* Love. Healing love is not fearful or possessive. It focuses on the presence and power of God, not on the illness. Healing empathy is not sympathy with the condition, but rather a quiet assurance of what the Divine Presence can do to restore wholeness of soul and body. Healing intent is vital, but it is not an "armamentarium." It is a realization of inner peace that releases a potential that is already present.

Faith, confidence, optimism, expectation, and trust are basic to effective prayer. The word "faith," however, has been a frequent source of confusion. It is used by different writers in a variety of ways. Faith is not blind belief, neither is it a set of doctrinal statements. Faith, at its core, is an inner quickening that is available to all as we turn our attention to the Divine Presence and are willing to see God's intent expressed and fulfilled in our everyday lives. In this book, we will consider faith as Jesus himself understood and used it in the context of the Gospel records.

"Thy will be done" is a good policy, if we can get past mistaken ideas of what God's will is. Divine Order always benefits us, when we are consciously attuned with what is true and beautiful and good. We find this to be the case through communion with the Indwelling God. As Emmet Fox wrote in *The Sermon on the Mount,* "True Christianity is an entirely positive influence. It comes into a man's life to enlarge and enrich it, to make it fuller and wider and better; never to restrict it."2

Prayer can be described as *a way of being* as well as *a way of doing.* There are many forms of prayer, but the essential need is to focus on the indwelling Presence which is love, light, wisdom, and peace. Jesus' instruction to "go into your closet" to pray is a metaphor, which does not mean that we take it less seriously. This figure of speech translates to "praying as in a closet shut off from distractions." It is an occasion for quiet communion with what he called *Abba,* an informal Aramaic word for "father," better translated as "daddy." It is the indwelling nature of God.

Dossey's statement that God belongs to everyone, and everyone belongs to God, is correct. Decades of experience in teaching and healing have shown that a few basic insights underlie our work, and that these can be found in a variety of spiritual traditions. A few basic discoveries by individuals, which cannot be precisely dated but were essential turning points, attest to the realities that we recognize.

At some undetermined date, Moses received the revelation of God as I AM THAT I AM (See Exodus, Chapter 3). This means that God's absolute and unconditioned nature is paramount. Reality is a fullness of divine ideas, and God is truly All-in-all. There is no *God-and.* In the Hebrew tradition, the prophets denounced any attempt by the Canaanites–as well as their own people–to worship idols or view God in limited terms. Because of their courage and spiritual insight, they deserve our everlasting honor and respect.

Jesus spent his boyhood in Galilee. As the New Testament scholar, Bruce Chilton, observes, given the parables in the Biblical record, he would have experienced the activity of God in the crops, fruit trees, and vineyards which were basic to his early experience. At an undetermined date, Jesus must have had *a flash of illumination* in which he recognized that the same law exists within our own consciousness. That is to say, the law that functions in the growth of crops is the same law of creative consciousness that functions through the thoughts, emotions, images, and beliefs of the human individual. We as individuals, in a manner of speaking, are co-creators with God; what we sow in mind we reap in experience. The same universal law functions in soul and body, working creatively from the inside out, from center to circumference and thence into the environment. This is one of the basic features of Jesus' healing consciousness. It is the essential truth affirmed in his seed parables.

That this flash of illumination occurred to an Oriental is interesting from the standpoint of Rocco Errico's commentary on Matthew 6:11, "Give us this day our daily bread," in the Lord's Prayer. He writes:

> The phrases–Let your will be, and Provide us our needful bread, (especially the expression "needful bread" which refers to supplying "needs") can be found in Hebrew "short prayers." Bread is treated with the utmost respect by Easterners because they literally, in the name of God, plant the precious seed, harvest, scatter the sheaves on the threshing floor, grind the grain into flour and bake their daily bread in a "God-centered" consciousness. The prayer for "needful bread from day to day" reflects a deep inner gratitude and acknowledgment of the Provider of all "good and perfect gifts."[3]

The early development of Hinduism is also relevant. In ancient times, the Brahmins, or priestly caste, performed elaborate rituals. They believed that these rites had to be performed in exact ways, for the order of the cosmos depended upon their success. If they did not do so, the universe would dissolve into chaos. Yet, at an undetermined time or times, some of the priests themselves discovered that the cosmos existed within their own consciousness, regardless of anything that was done or failed to be done outwardly, and that therefore the rituals were unnecessary. It was at this point that Hindu philosophy and yoga were born.

What is relevant here is that the cosmos in all its immensity, both invisible and visible, is indeed implanted within us, and is accessible to our own consciousness. Jacob Boehme and other mystics were right about this. Metaphysical teachers who declare, "Whatever is, is here," do not exaggerate. If it were not so, we could not even imagine the cosmos as current science and astronomy conceive it to be. The Word does indeed become flesh. The human cell is the epitome of the cosmos.

How these basic insights relate to the healing ministry will become clearer as we turn to Jesus of Nazareth and review the records of his healing activity. The author has a strong Christian orientation and commitment. Yet he realizes that what he is writing about is bigger than any one religion or spiritual tradition. Whether one considers Jesus to be a god, a man, fully God and fully man, or holds to some other theological view, remember that Christ is more than a man, even Jesus. Christ is our life (Colossians 3:4), as well as the life of Jesus. Thus, the Healing Christ has a double meaning, bring both a person (Jesus of Nazareth) and a collective principle and reality (Christ in us all).

Note Jesus' assuring statement in John 14:12: "Truly, truly, I say to you, he who believes in me will also do the works that I do, and greater works than these will he do."

Chapter 1

The Man With an Unclean Spirit

21And they went into Capernaum, and immediately on the sabbath he entered the synagogue and taught. 22And they were astonished at his teaching, for he taught them as one who had authority, and not as the scribes. 23And immediately there was in their synagogue a man with an unclean spirit; 24and he cried out, "What have you to do with us, Jesus of Nazareth? Have you come to destroy us? I know who you are, the Holy One of God." 25But Jesus rebuked him, saying, "Be silent, and come out of him!" 26And the unclean spirit, convulsing him and crying with a loud voice, came out of him. 27And they were all amazed, so that they questioned among themselves, saying, "What is this? A new teaching! With authority he commands even the unclean spirits, and they obey him." 28And at once his fame spread everywhere throughout all the surrounding region of Galilee.
–Mark 1:21-28 (parallel passage: Luke 4:31-37)

Oral traditions regarding Jesus' sayings and deeds, in the early beginnings of what became the Christian movement, were strictly accurate. Writing them down, however, was an invitation to change them. This is the opposite of what we expect in the modern Western World. We assume that writing something down freezes its form, whereas passing it on by word of mouth is an invitation to revise and embellish. In both the Near East and in India, however, and in parts of Africa, oral tradition is reliable and memories are trained in ways that are rarely known or practiced in the West. Even great scholars, especially in the New Testament field, have seen things backwards because of their own

1

cultural biases.

A basic question is: Did Jesus view himself as an exorcist? Or was this added to the tradition at a later time? Our experience in New Thought weighs heavily in favor of defining "unclean spirits" as clusters of negative, destructive thoughts, emotions, images, and beliefs. Also, addictions of every kind are "demonic" to those who are enslaved by them. Our experience does not confirm the existence of separate entities that roam at large and try to possess given individuals. We look for the functioning of *a universal science* underlying the healing ministry. It is more natural to believe that whole-making, in soul and body, does not violate the law of our being, but fulfills it.

At the same time, we are reluctant to decide anything on the basis of dogma, and are inclined to examine all sides of an issue. We will strive to do this as we examine Mark 1:21-28.

The image in 1:21 is symbolic. Jesus enters the synagogue and teaches there. The Greek verb translated "to teach" [*didasko*] is in the imperfect tense, implying continuous action. That is to say, as soon as he entered the building he began to teach and continued to do so for some time. In the same way, the Indwelling Christ is ready to move into our own awareness, to instruct all the thoughts of the mind and the affections of the heart. Here is the Source of healing, waiting to be released and manifested through us.

"They were astonished at his teaching, for he taught them as one who had authority [*exousia*], and not as the scribes." (1:22) The Romans used the term *exousia* for authority in a legal sense, meaning power delegated under the authority of their own government. The American concept of equal justice under law was beyond the Roman ideal. The Romans did, however, try to dispense rights and privileges according to merit as they understood it.

In the New Testament, and in the idiom of the times in a wider sense, being a child of God not only denoted kinship, but also empowerment. For example, John 1:12 declares: "To all who received him, who believed in his name, he gave power [again, *exousia*] to become children of God." Jesus said, "Love your enemies and pray for those who persecute you, *so that you may be sons of your Father* who is in heaven. (Matthew 5:44-45) In other words, according to Jesus' frame of reference, loving and praying for our enemies is not only Godlike; it is empowering as well.

This divine authority, however, is not exercised through personal will, but by yielding control of our inner nature to the Mind of God and His ideas. The term implies this, for it is based on two other Greek words, *ex* [out of, from] and *ousa* [the present participle of *eimi*, the verb "to be"]. The root meaning of *exousia*, then, is "out of being or substance." In New Testament times, it meant "power, capacity, mastery, might, freedom, strength, jurisdiction."

This is a way of saying that healing potential inheres in the universal I AM or Christ, and can unfold through the consciousness of the individual. The power to release healing, for self and others, however, requires a willing and receptive attitude. Affirm:

I AM ONE WITH THE SPIRITUAL UNIVERSE. COMPLETE WHOLENESS, HARMONY, WELL-BEING ARE REAL NOW. I RECEIVE AND RELEASE THE HEALING ACTION OF GOD IN MIND, BODY, AND AFFAIRS.

GOD'S LAW OF HARMONY AND HEALTH NOW GOVERNS MY MIND AND BODY, AND I AM HEALED. I

SHOW FORTH THIS TRUTH IN HAPPY, HEALTHY, AND PRODUCTIVE WAYS.

"And immediately there was in the synagogue a man with an unclean spirit." (1:23)

This suggests certain questions. For example:

How does the healing activity of Jesus relate to "unclean spirits" and their removal?
Can unclean spirits be made "clean"?
What are "unclean spirits" in the first place? Are they independent entities? Or are they clusters of negative images and emotions that take control of some people on a subconscious level?

Unclean spirits or demons, are never described in the Bible. Nowhere does it say, for example, that a demon is three feet high, red or green, sporting horns on its head, or carrying a pitchfork. The Gospel of Luke gives far greater emphasis to demon possession, but the Gospel of Mark is earlier and in the main more accurate in its healing records than Luke. If the author of Luke was a physician, as is sometimes claimed, he was certainly a peculiar one – even for his own era – with his belief that demons cause disease.

The term "evil spirits" is still used in the 21st Century by some church leaders and psychics. This, however, is more of a scare tactic than a serious effort to bring clarity. Still, we must concede the likelihood that in ancient times, most people believed in the existence of evil spirits. Also, in the interests of fairness, it must be acknowledged that people in Asian and other traditional cultures tend to be more open to the spirit world than modern westerners living in Europe or in the United States.

On the other hand, the Aramaic tradition of the text uses a term for unclean spirits that does not necessarily imply possession by an outside entity. George Lamsa, who knew remaining pockets of the Aramaic language and culture first-hand, wrote:

> The Aramaic words *rokha tamtha* mean "the unclean spirit," a person who is unruly, insane, or has an evil inclination. In the East, any wrong inclination is considered unclean, whether it be a person, food, speech, or teaching.

> Medical terms were unknown in biblical days. The people who suffered mentally were considered possessed by an evil inclination, or mentally disturbed.. The term "spirit" in Aramaic also means "inclination," "rheumatism," "temper," "pride," or "a person."[1]

Also, note that the man's entry into the synagogue went unchallenged. He would not have been allowed in if the people had believed him to be possessed by an outside entity. According to the ceremonial concepts of Judaism, he would then have been "unclean." His presence would, in turn, have rendered the whole synagogue and everyone in it unclean. Also, in the Gospel accounts, Jesus is *only once* specifically asked to perform an exorcism. This is the case of the Syrophoenician woman (Mark 7:24-30, cf. Matthew 15:21-28), which occurred in Gentile territory where people were less familiar with Jewish practices.

It is uncertain how much of the man's ravings in Mark 1:24 reflect authentic memories. Such ravings, or others similar to it, could plausibly reflect emotional and perhaps even psychotic confusion. The electrifying teachings and actions of Jesus could easily have activated long and deeply repressed emotions in this man. These could have come to the surface in a sudden outburst, as a frenzied reaction. This is not at all strange; serious counseling sessions, whether individual or group, sometimes draw out a patient's repressed emotional contents. Mark 1:26, "convulsing him and crying out with a loud voice," fits this interpretation. Later, if a writer wanted to depict Jesus fighting and casting out unclean spirits, it would not have been too great an extension of the memories of this event to place it in this context.

Nevertheless, according to Mark 1:25 (which may or may not be part of the original tradition), Jesus shouted *phimotheti*. It means "shut up," and both the Greek and the Aramaic traditions of the text agree that "to shut the mouth" is the underlying meaning. But more than that, Greek magicians used the term to make a person incapable of doing harm. Jesus could have used this term not because he viewed himself as an exorcist, but merely because the man had a belief structure that took this sort of thing seriously. It may have served to prevent an immediate crisis, such as damage to persons or property. It would also have supported the patient's underlying hope that Jesus could free him of his affliction. The account is clear that he was healed.

Physicians and practitioners of all schools will, in most situations, do whatever it takes to bring about a cure. Healing is both a science and an art. Where there is all science and no art, there is a lack of rapport with those needing help. Many people in the modern medical profession have serious concerns here. On the other hand, where there is all art and no science, we find the work of conjurors and charlatans, a concern both then and now for everyone in the healing field.

Another question has been asked: Are reports of earth-bound spirits correct? That is, are there any people, when they die physically, who believe they are still "alive" and thus fail to advance to their appropriate plane? The answer is yes, there are some. Also, there are people who do rescue work, to persuade these souls to go on to claim the new opportunities that await them in other realms of eternal life.

According to some observers, more is claimed, namely, that some of these excarnates intrude upon and attach their etheric bodies to the bodies of people still in the flesh. Is this correct? Not in this writer's experience, but this does not prove the case one way or the other.

Nevertheless, if such intrusions actually occur, the offending entities are in as great a need of help as those they are intruding upon. They are not to be condemned, but to be coaxed and encouraged to complete their journey to their appropriate plane.

God is all-powerful, and we are not to fear opposition from organized powers of darkness. If they ever existed, they would have destroyed themselves utterly long ago. This can be seen by considering examples on this plane. The Third Reich lasted only 12 years, and Adolf Hitler's dream of a National Socialist Millennium died in the ashes. The Soviet Union dissolved in chaos after about 70 years.

In summary, then, the evidence can be taken three ways: (1) Jesus may have viewed himself as an exorcist, casting our unclean spirits; (2) He may have played the role of one in certain cases, letting God do the work through his healing consciousness while acting *as if* he were casting out unclean spirits; (3) The oral tradition, when reduced to writing, may have been reworked to picture Jesus as an exorcist, though he was not one and never pretended to be.[2]

It is understandable that the Followers of the Way, as the earliest Christians thought of themselves, would have viewed persecutions as demonic. In a metaphoric sense, they were just that. During the reign of King Herod Agrippa in Palestine (41-44

A.D.), the Romans and the Pharisees did, in fact, join forces in trying to eradicate the early Jesus movement. Herod Agrippa, a grandson of Herod the Great, evidently believed that he, and not Jesus, was the Messiah. This persecution would have been the occasion for departing from the oral tradition, and for beginning to depict Jesus *in writing* as casting out evil spirits, instead of merely healing the sick. An urtext of the Gospel of Mark, written by an unknown author, could well have been composed *during this period*. Later, about 70 A.D., John Mark would have revised and expanded it to become the gospel which today carries his name.

Also, it is widely accepted that the Gospel of Mark has the basic traits of a play. In order for a drama to have a plot, it must have an adversary of some kind, even if the adversary must be created or at least placed in a different light.

However one may view the historical background, there should be agreement that the Christian ministry has a definite calling to "cast out" fear, hate, lust, greed, resentment, and self-pity. These "unclean spirits," while they continue to obsess an individual, can only lead to discordant actions and conditions, disease, and premature death.

Any cluster or fixation of negative images can be cast out. In mediating such soul healings, we experience the Healing Christ in a most powerful way, bringing about wholeness and deliverance where it is most needed.

The potential for healing is always present, for one can identify with the I AM or Indwelling Christ which has no limitation. This is the one focus of attention that cannot be made to excess; for the Christ includes everyone and everything within its scope. It is the healthy totality, which functions to balance and reintegrate disparate elements within the psyche. The Healing

Christ can be affirmed as follows:

I IDENTIFY WITH THE INDWELLING CHRIST. I HAVE THE MIND OF CHRIST.

MY SOUL IS BALANCED, BOTH CONSCIOUSLY AND SUBCONSCIOUSLY. ALL IMAGES AND EMOTIONS ARE RESTORED TO DIVINE ORDER.

ALL THE THOUGHTS OF MY MIND AND HEART, VERBAL AND VISUAL, ARE BROUGHT INTO RIGHT RELATION AND PROPORTION WITH EACH OTHER, IN THE HEALING CHRIST.

I AM NOT BOUND BY FALSE BELIEFS. I AM FREE WITH THE FREEDOM OF SPIRIT.

I AM DELIVERED OUT OF ERROR, AND INTO THE FREE LIFE OF A CHILD OF GOD, IN THE NAME AND THROUGH THE POWER OF THE INDWELLING CHRIST.

As we continue to work with the laws of the spiritual kingdom, we do more than solve specific problems. We discover that life is more than a series of mishaps, and a series of solutions to correct them. By being the Christ actively in thought, word, and deed, we become, even as Jesus, active lights of the world, cities set on a hill that cannot be hid.

Chapter 2

Peter's Mother-in-law

29And immediately he left the synagogue, and entered the house of Simon and Andrew, with James and John. 30Now Simon's mother-in-law lay sick with a fever, and immediately they told him of her. 31And he came and took her by the hand and lifted her up, and the fever left her; and she served them.
–Mark 1:29-31 (parallel passages: Matthew 8:14-15; Luke 4:38-39)

We, like Simon's (Peter's) mother-in-law, need to be lifted up in spirit. Lying prone, and then being lifted up by Jesus, is an image of awakening from a limiting and discordant belief system into the light of true understanding. The Christ Mind enters our awareness, restoring wholeness to our souls and bodies.

The feverish woman is an image of our souls while in a process of purgation or purification.1 In a permanent healing, the Healing Christ moves into our subconscious phase of mind to heal, harmonize, and adjust. We aid this process by maintaining positive images, and using affirmative statements, such as the following:

THE CHRIST MIND ILLUMINES AND GUIDES ME. I WALK IN THE LIGHT.

THE SPIRIT WITHIN ME QUICKENS MY UNDERSTANDING. I KNOW THE TRUTH THAT FREES ME FROM ALL SENSE OF LIMITATION AND BONDAGE.

11

THERE IS ONE PERFECT SPIRIT OF INTEGRITY
WORKING IN AND THROUGH ME, EXPRESSING ITS
HARMONIOUS NATURE IN MIND, BODY, AND AFFAIRS.

Jesus *sometimes* used the laying on of hands as a channel of
healing. This was not unusual in ancient times. To this day,
people in many cultures do it. It is also significant, however, that
Jesus sometimes did *not* touch the patient physically. The
obvious conclusion is that touching the patient was helpful in
some instances, but not essential to his approach. This suggests
a policy that we might adopt for ourselves.

There are two reasons why touching the patient can make a
difference. For one thing, it increases his or her confidence in
being healed. A tangible act that strengthens the *expectation* of
healing is helpful in and of itself, for people tend to receive what
they expect. This is not, however, the whole point. Actual
energy flows through the healer's hands and arms. This energy
is often experienced as heat, but it is much more than that. It
tends to balance and harmonize the energy patterns surrounding
the client's body. It can make a difference toward restoring a
harmonious state in the body and also, to a degree, in the psyche.

In our own times, two women have pioneered what has
become a widespread trend in the nursing field, *therapeutic
touch*. Note, however, that in their practice, the healer need not
touch the patient's skin, but can have beneficial effects while
bringing the hands within a few inches of the patient's body.
These women are Dolores Krieger, PhD, and Dora Kunz.[2]
Through clinical experience, they have demonstrated that the
visible body does have invisible energy fields surrounding it. By
so doing, they are helping to dispel the myth that our true being
ends with our skins. Their work is valid science in its clinical
tradition. It is not, as some have falsely claimed, a form of
campus radicalism or pernicious thought control.

Using touch, or therapeutic touch, is not a priority in New Thought practice. What is striking, however, in reading Dolores Krieger's books is the extent to which the positive feelings of those who use therapeutic touch are the same as the positive feelings of New Thought practitioners. Krieger, Kunz, and their colleagues tell of gaining new purpose in life through their ability to help those who seek them out. They tell of peace and serenity, a more optimistic view of life, a renewal of confidence, and uplifting feelings of love and personal warmth. This adds powerfully to the impression that practitioners of therapeutic touch are helping in their own way to fulfill God's positive intentions, just as we are.

Many New Thought practitioners have serious reservations about using touch of either variety. The core of our method, after all, is affirmative prayer and the realization of oneness with God. One valid concern is that they may inadvertently narrow their own goals in healing practice to a "quick fix." They rightly conclude that what is really needed is to help people to release the activity of God in *all* areas of their lives. Healing a headache or a sick stomach is well and good, but it is a far cry from being transformed by the renewing of one's mind in Christ. Dedicated healers are also reluctant to risk making patients dependent on their physical presence. These are serious concerns that are not to be dismissed lightly.

On the other hand, we find Jesus of Nazareth touching some patients, without it placing any limits on his effectiveness with others, in other situations. Therefore, following the same policy should not be an insuperable challenge for us. We should be able to use touch when appropriate, and still in every case remain attuned to the Infinite Whole in Its healing perfection.

Unfortunately, there are people in every profession who have not learned to control their own sexuality, and this can have tragic consequences when working with patients or clients of the opposite sex. People who have tendencies in this direction would do well to withdraw from public work altogether, unless and until they are healed of their problems. It is hard to imagine how anyone could act from unclean motives and be an effective practitioner.

It is really not difficult to raise or lower body temperature, and without drugs. Hypnotists do this through the use of suggestion. With biofeedback equipment, most people can learn to raise and lower body temperature at will. The person holds a thermometer, and is told to feel a hand becoming hot or cold. With practice, this can be done without the thermometer.

When spiritual consciousness is at work, however—with or without touch—body temperature will tend to return to an optimum level whether it is above *or* below this level. Thus, if two people are prayed for affirmatively, one with a temperature of 95 and the other with a temperature of 102, both will tend to return to 98.6F with the *same* affirmative prayer. This is significant because it shows a divinely natural, orderly pattern at work toward healing.

The healing works of Jesus often occurred among groups of friendly and expectant people. This reflects, in part, the mechanics of suggestion. The terms *hypnosis* and *suggestion*, however, are far from expressing the essential nature of Jesus' healing practice. It is not that one mind is influencing many other minds, and is in turn being influenced by them. Rather, in group situations of this kind—then and now—there is a collective realization of One Mind, of oneness and love and harmony. That is to say, the essence of spiritual healing, as taught and practiced by Jesus, is not at all in the nature of separate minds contacting and controlling one another. Rather, it is in the realization of the Unity of Being. *There is a consciousness of oneness with the healee and with God, coupled with a definite intent that healing take place.* This consciousness is expressed in the Gospel of John: "In that day, you will know that I am in my Father, and you in me, and I in you." (John 14:20) "I in them and thou in me, that they may become perfectly one." (John 17:23)

Hypnotism works by suspending the patient's will, and by injecting a flow of imagery, verbal and visual, *from the hypnotist's own psyche.* This changes the subconscious mind of the patient to a degree, though results are usually temporary. The hypnotist may also, without intending to do so, transfer *discordant* images into the patient's psyche. Using Jesus' methods, the flow of imagery is *released from within the individual needing help,* thus also changing the subconscious phase of mind. In the latter case, however, the change is natural to the patient. Being indigenous to the patient's own psyche, it is always more or less permanent.

A spiritually mature counselor or practitioner finds it as distasteful to exercise personal control over a patient as would Jesus himself. Carl G. Jung, founder of depth psychology, noted: "I gave up hypnotic treatment for this very reason, because I did not want to impose my will on others. I wanted the healing process to grow out of the patient's own personality, not from suggestions by me that would have only a passing effect."[3]

Returning to the Biblical record, there is too little data for a medical doctor to venture a diagnosis, although malaria was not uncommon and has been suggested. Fevers lead to the destruction of toxins and undesirable bacteria. Yet there are cases in which a fever is so high that it becomes life-threatening. Then, of course, swift action must be taken whether medical or non-medical. Also, if a fever continues for a long time, the problem is not being handled effectively. One of the subtleties of the Greek text, not translated into English, is that the patient's fever had continued for a long time. "Lay sick" translates *katakeimai*, which we find in the imperfect tense, emphasizing the lengthy and continuous nature of the fever.

Eliminating a fever can be accomplished either through spiritual practice or through hypnotism. To eliminate a fever through hypnosis, however, is risky. The symptoms will be suppressed, but the toxins will remain and the undesirable bacteria will proliferate. This illustrates a basic challenge with using hypnosis: It must be very specific in order to work, but by being too specific, it tends to suppress symptoms, but not to solve problems *as a whole*.

When body temperature is returned to a normal range by spiritual methods, this problem does not occur. Not only do symptoms disappear, but the entire situation is often healed at the same time. Touching a patient (or therapeutic touch, as practiced by Krieger and Kunz), may seem a purely physical procedure, but in practice, the consciousness of the patient is often harmonized as well as bringing physical cure or improvement. Nevertheless, touch has only an ancillary role, as it did when Jesus acted to bring healing to Peter's mother-in-law. Christ Consciousness does the essential work.

Chapter 3

Lepers Cleansed

40And a leper came to him beseeching him, and kneeling said to him, "If you will, you can make me clean." 41Moved with pity, he stretched out his hand and touched him, and said to him, "I will; be clean." 42And immediately the leprosy left him, and he was made clean. 43And he sternly charged him, and sent him away at once, 44and said to him, "See that you say nothing to any one; but go, show yourself to the priest, and offer for your cleansing what Moses commanded, for a proof to the people." 45But he went out and began to talk freely about it, and to spread the news, so that Jesus could no longer openly enter a town, but was out in the country; and people came to him from every quarter.
–Mark 1:40-45 (parallel passages: Matthew 8:1-4; Luke 5:12-16)

A fragment of a lost gospel probably records the same event, though it could represent a different event. This early manuscript, consisting of three fragments, is known collectively as Egerton Papyrus 2. It includes the following:

> And behold, a leper, coming to him, said, "Master Jesus, journeying with lepers and eating with them in the inn, I also became a leper. If, therefore, you will, I can be made clean." The Lord then said to him, "I will; be clean." And immediately the leprosy left him, and the Lord said to him, "Go and show yourselves to the priests."[1]

Though we will call the patient "the leper" for convenience sake, there is serious doubt that he had what today is called

17

leprosy. The Greek word *lepra* appears in the text. In the Old Testament Septuagint (the translation made in Alexandria from the original Hebrew into Greek), *lepra* always meant leprosy. This, however, mistranslates Hebrew words for eczema, psoriasis, and the like, found in Leviticus, Chapter 13. The New Testament uses the term *lepra*. Greek healers contemporary with Jesus used this same term to refer to a variety of skin conditions. Many skin conditions are difficult to diagnose, even by skilled modern physicians. So we cannot be certain about the nature of the illness.

Egerton 2, however, provides a clue that it could have been leprosy. The man states that he traveled with lepers and ate with them, and the disease is contagious with prolonged exposure.

Both sources agree that the patient was healed immediately. This is remarkable in itself, whatever the diagnosis. Skin conditions of many types, including and especially stress-related conditions, are notoriously difficult to cure.

People who were labeled lepers suffered and became disabled, but the social consequences were even worse. They became outcasts, rejected by friends and even their own families. They were usually driven from their homes and went to dwell with other victims apart from society. They were permitted to walk about only if they shouted, "unclean, unclean." This kind of negative affirmation certainly didn't help their own self-image, but it did serve to keep people at a distance. According to Egerton 2, the lepers apparently concealed their condition while patronizing a public inn.

To fully appreciate the dire consequences of being labeled a leper, whether correctly or not, we need to understand something of the Jewish concepts of ceremonial cleanness and uncleanness. *A key point is that cleanness was associated with God and life, and uncleanness with disintegration and death.* Within this religious system, a leper believed himself to be literally under God's curse. Leprosy was more than a symbol of sin; people believed that God sometimes punished sin by afflicting a person with the disease. This belief, in and of itself, made recovery rare and difficult. For what man or woman can prevail against the power and will of God? From what we know today of psychology, it is apparent that the conviction of sin and guilt would have effectively blocked the natural healing process, while also increasing stress and thus making the condition worse–a vicious cycle.

The healing Presence of God is such that even within this negative belief system, a leper occasionally recovered. The Jewish priesthood followed elaborate procedures for examining a person in this situation, which are outlined in Leviticus 14:1-32. This was not in any sense a healing ritual, but a certification that healing had already taken place. If all evidence of the disease was gone, the priests certified the person to be cleansed. This also restored him to his family and community. Jesus told the man to go to the priests and to request the prescribed ritual.

Let us consider the insights behind Jesus' actions. *The first is to recognize that the will of God, the pattern of His activity, is health and wholeness.* The very nature of God is harmony and perfection. God would no more produce disease than a waterfall would reverse its course. Healing is never contrary to the will of God.

The leper did not doubt that God had the power to heal him through Jesus. He was uncertain that God was *willing* to have him well. For according to popular belief, and even ecclesiastical sanction, God had rejected and cursed all lepers.

Jesus did not hesitate to be a channel for healing. He answered, "I will; be clean." Let us look at what this means for people today. Jesus here symbolizes the Indwelling Christ, and the leper represents the personal self under a felt burden of sin. The Christ "touches" us both consciously and subconsciously, which restores our sense of being spiritually clean and one with God. This means more than healing a specific condition (though that is not excluded). A personal sense of sin, weakness, and disease can be rooted out and destroyed. It can be replaced by a spiritual sense of Self, which is one with God.

Affirm:

I ACCEPT THE TRUTH THAT GOD'S WILL IS EXPRESSED IN ALL THAT IS HEALTHY, WHOLE, AND HARMONIOUS.

I AM MADE CLEAN AND WHOLE, THROUGH THE PRESENCE AND POWER OF THE INDWELLING CHRIST.

THE DIVINE PRESENCE IS FOREVER MAKING ALL THINGS NEW. I AM RENEWED AND RESTORED IN MIND AND BODY.

THROUGH THE SPIRIT OF GOD IN ME, I AM NOW RESPONDING TO HIS HEALING LOVE.

The translation of Mark states in error that Jesus was "moved with pity." The Greek word (*splagchnizomai*) means basically *to have a "gut feeling" of compassion*. It does not imply that Jesus felt sorry for him. If the translators, learned scholars that they were, had practical experience in the healing ministry, they would have understood that the word "pity" is clearly out of context. Pity never healed anyone, and is actually destructive to a healing consciousness, tending to reinforce rather than to cure an illness. Jesus' compassion was positive and empowering, for he knew what God could do for the one who asked for help.

If we found a man who was caught in quicksand, we would not jump in with him. We would throw him a rope.

Many of the healed people in the Gospel records no doubt had periods of soul-searching before they asked the Great Physician for help. The results, though often instantaneous, came when they released their anxiety and let the action of God take over.

It is well to affirm:

THE ONE PERFECT MIND OF GOD NEVER CREATED A DISEASE.

ANY ADVERSE CONDITION IN MY LIFE THEREFORE HAS NO RIGHT TO EXIST, AND NO CLAIM ON MY CONSCIOUSNESS.

THE PERFECT MIND THAT CREATED ME, MADE ME OUT OF ITS OWN PERFECTION.

I AM RADIANT WITH THIS TRUTH OF MY BEING. THIS IS THE TRUTH OF ME, AND IT SETS ME FREE. I LET GO AND LET GOD.

The leper no doubt had much fear. Jesus touched him, to assure him of healing and also to show him that he had no fear of the condition. In this way, the patient's fear also dissolved, a basic step toward healing in his case.

This directly reversed the conventional "wisdom" of the time–a trait of some of Jesus' parables, too. According to the Levitical Law, when he touched the leper, he himself became unclean and was transferred to the realm of death. What happened, however, was that when Jesus touched the man, that man became clean and thus was restored to the realm of life. In the same way, Divine ideas are stronger than negative beliefs, health is stronger than sickness, and love is stronger than fear.

When Jesus gained the realization that life, humanity, and the cosmos are whole and undivided in the Omnipresence of God, the traditional purity laws of Judaism were irretrievably shattered in his belief system. It no longer made any difference to him whether or not a fish had fins and scales. It no longer made any difference whether water was stored in a clay pot or a stone pot.

The concepts of clean and unclean were not, however, removed from Jesus' thinking altogether. They were, rather, transferred to the realm of *consciousness* where they really belong (which means infinitely more than "conscience" alone). What is *clean* was seen to be the activity of God through the consciousness of the individual, when God's ideas are being faithfully expressed and demonstrated. What is *unclean* was seen to be any distortion of consciousness into chaos and negativity, which denied the supremacy of God's kingdom. Jesus was utterly frank in this respect. He declared:

> "What comes out of a man is what defiles a man. For from within, out of the heart of man, come evil thoughts, fornication, theft, murder, adultery, coveting, wickedness, deceit, licentiousness, envy, slander, pride, foolishness. All these evil things come from within, and they defile a man." (Mark 7:20-23)

When you have been healed, you then need to continue to think, speak, and act in positive ways as befits a spiritual being, a son or daughter of God. As Emmet Fox declared, "Change your mind and keep it changed." Note–and this is extremely important–that Jesus typically gave his patients *something specific to do*, to express their trust in a positive way. As already noted, he sent the healed man to the temple priests to be certified as cleansed. This would have reinforced the man's confidence that his healing was not only in keeping with God's will, but permanent. Jesus, being consciously one with Omnipresent Life and having no fear of death (which he understood as illusory), disregarded the Levitical Law. In touching this patient, he had specifically broken that law. Nevertheless, Jesus knew that the ritual was impressive to those who believed in it, and that it could be decisive in reassuring him that he would *remain* healthy.

Affirm:

I APPROACH LIFE WITH CONFIDENCE AND STRENGTH, KNOWING THAT GOD THE GOOD IS IN CHARGE.

I AM AN ILLUMINED CHILD OF GOD, FILLED WITH THE SPIRIT OF DIVINE LOVE AND WISDOM, BY WHICH I AM GUIDED IN ALL MY WAYS, AND LED INTO THAT WHICH IS FOR MY HIGHEST GOOD.

People rarely become sick in isolation. Therefore, heed this warning: *When you have had a major healing, do not associate or talk with scoffers or others of a negative frame of mind.* Think and visualize cleanness, as Jesus came to understand its true meaning. After he released healing for the man in question, "He sternly charged him, and sent him away at once, and said to him, 'See that you say nothing to any one.'" It must have created quite a stir. The translators are too polite here; according to Mark's dramatic Greek, Jesus shouted at him and perhaps even removed him physically from the crowd. The Greek word translated "sent him away" is *ekballo*, which means "to throw out."

An individual can be talked out of a healing that has already occurred. Jesus saw the possibility of a relapse, and took decisive action to separate the cleansed man from the crowd. He wanted the man to go directly to the temple priests in Jerusalem, and then to quietly return home, wherever that might be.

The Gospel of Luke includes another account, of the healing of ten lepers:

11On the way to Jerusalem he was passing along between Samaria and Galilee. 12And as he entered a village, he was met by ten lepers, who stood at a distance 13and lifted up their voices and said, "Jesus, Master, have mercy on us." 14When he saw them, he said to them, "Go and show yourselves to the priests." And as they went they were cleansed. 15Then one of them, when he saw that he was healed, turned back, praising God with a loud voice; 16and he fell on his face at Jesus' feet, giving him thanks. Now he was a Samaritan. 17Then said Jesus, "Were not ten cleansed? Where are the nine? 18Was no one found to return and give praise to God except this foreigner? 19And he said to him, "Rise and go your way; your faith has made you well."
–Luke 17:11-19

As in the case of the single leper, Jesus told them to go and show themselves to the priests. He did not touch these ten people. He told them to go on their way with an attitude of trust, to the effect that they were healed. "And as they went they were cleansed."

We are naturally inclined to think more highly of the Samaritan who returned to thank Jesus and praise God. This goes beyond the issue of common decency. Spiritual consciousness is inherently grateful because it is based on the oneness we have with God and the cosmos. We should not, however, be too hard on the other nine. They merely took Jesus at his word when he told them to *go* in a spirit of trust.

This text is part of an allegorical journey in the Gospel of Luke, which Jesus takes to Jerusalem, beginning with Luke 9:51. That the journey was not a literal one is obvious by the lack of identifying place names along the way. Whether the healings in Luke 17:11-19 are taken to be literal or allegorical, or both, however, the action of the Samaritan is a lesson of great importance. Praise and gratitude are more than proper attitudes. In a practical therapeutic sense, praise and gratitude produce physical changes that speed up the healing process. Gloom and ingratitude block or at least retard it.

The psalmist tradition of praise is beautiful and uplifting, and it is also healing to the soul and body. For example, Psalms 103:1-5, in the majestic cadences of the King James Version, declares:

Bless the Lord, O my soul: and all that is within me, bless his holy name.
Bless the Lord, O my soul, and forget not all his benefits:
Who forgiveth all thine iniquities; who healeth all thy diseases;
Who redeemth thy life from destruction; who crowneth thee with loving kindness and tender mercies;
Who satisfieth thy mouth with good things; so that thy youth is renewed like the eagle's."

Chapter 4

Paralytic Carried by Four Men

1And when he returned to Capernaum after some days, it was reported that he was at home. 2And many were gathered together, so that there was no longer room for them, not even about the door; and he was preaching the word to them. 3And they came, bringing to him a paralytic carried by four men. 4And when they could not get near him because of the crowd, they removed the roof above him; and when they had made an opening, they let down the pallet on which the paralytic lay. 5And when Jesus saw their faith, he said to the paralytic, "My son, your sins are forgiven." 6Now some of the scribes were sitting there, questioning in their hearts, 7"Why does this man speak thus? It is blasphemy! Who can forgive sins but God alone?" 8And immediately Jesus, perceiving in his spirit that they thus questioned within themselves, said to them, "Why do you question thus in your hearts? 9Which is easier, to say to the paralytic, 'Your sins are forgiven,' or to say, 'Rise, take up your pallet and walk'? 10But that you may know that the Son of man has authority on earth to forgive sins"–he said to the paralytic– 11I say to you, rise, take up your pallet and go home." 12And he rose, and immediately took up the pallet and went out before them all; so that they were all amazed and glorified God, saying, "We never saw anything like this!"
–Mark 2:1-12 (parallel passages: Matthew 9:1-8; Luke 5:17-26)

Enthusiastic disciples jammed the house where Jesus stayed in Capernaum. Not only the inside of the building, but also the doorway, was impassable. Four men came carrying a paralyzed man on a pallet. Due to the crowds, they could not bring him to Jesus through the doorway. So they made a hole in the roof, and lowered the pallet on ropes to the room below.

A hole in the roof? Yes, for in ancient Capernaum, the roofs of houses consisted of a grid of wood with grass or straw placed over it. Thus, to make a hole in the roof would not have caused an unwarranted amount of damage. Such holes were quite easy to make, and simple to repair.

Also, the pallets which the common people used as beds were not heavy. They consisted of a wooden frame and a quilt. One could have served quite well as a stretcher. It did not require superhuman strength to carry it.

The dynamics of this narrative can best be interpreted in light of its four basic steps:

(1) *paralysis*–the patient could not walk. Since Jesus called him "son," he would have been young, probably a teenager, but already a man according to Jewish custom. Jesus was a comparatively young leader.

(2) *guilt*–For whatever reason, the man had done something wrong, thought he had done so, or held a mental picture of doing wrong.

(3) *forgiveness*–He accepted Jesus' assurance of being forgiven. This involves an inward process of "letting go."

(4) *healing*–He got up, walked, and took his pallet home with him.

The scribes who were present, questioning Jesus in their hearts, were not people whom one would recommend as pastoral counselors or even as ordinary psychologists. I am reminded of a young Baptist who tried to drown out his anger by heavy drinking. He had a desire to inflict bodily harm on another young man; this, plus his drinking of alcohol which was in defiance of his early training, led to a strong guilt complex. He then became paralyzed, for which the medical profession could find no objective cause. Later, he gave up alcohol and sincerely forgave both himself and his former enemy. He also, unexpectedly, recovered his ability to walk.

The Biblical narrative does not require any particular doctrine of sin and redemption in order to understand it. Moral wrong often leads to physical disease and malfunction, but not in every case. What we find portrayed here is the bitter fruit of hostility toward some person or situation. Instead of overt acts toward the object of his hostility, however, the individual unconsciously diverts it toward his own body. This makes it impossible for him to injure his enemy, but does nothing to deal with the sense of guilt which hate produces. Jesus, in counseling him, enabled him to solve his spiritual problem. The inner healing made the outer result not only possible, but certain.

Human consciousness, as a whole, has seen improvement in the past 2000 years. Some things haven't changed, however, and even in ancient times, there were people who contained their hostility by diverting it against their own bodies. An ancient work from roughly the same period, *The Testaments of the Twelve Patriarchs*, tells the story of Simeon's anger against Judah, who sold Joseph into slavery and thus spared Joseph's life. This account is fiction, but the *Testaments*–a point usually missed by scholars–are quite advanced in the psychological insights that they offer. The unknown author probably wrote a fictionalized account of an actual person. The Testament of Simeon 2:11-13 reads:

"But when I heard it, I was furious with Judah because he had let him [Joseph] go away alive. For five months I was angry at him. The Lord bound my hands and feet, however, and thus prevented my hands from performing their deeds because for seven days, my right hand became partly withered. I knew, children, that this had happened to me because of Joseph, so I repented and wept. Then I prayed to the Lord God that my hand might be restored and that I might refrain from every defilement and grudge and from all folly, for I knew that I had contemplated an evil deed in the sight of the Lord and of Jacob, my father, on account of Joseph, my brother, because of my envying him."[1]

Forgiveness is the key issue here. When we are willing to forgive ourselves and others, this inner change frees us from the past and empowers us to make progress in every area of life.

The Greek word for sin in the text is *hamartia*. It does not necessarily refer to moral or ethical wrong. It actually means an error, a wrong state of mind or soul. It is, in turn, from *hamartano*, an archery term meaning "to miss the mark." Jesus is not only referring to evildoing, but also to false and negative patterns of thinking and of image-making in the mind and heart. This "misses the mark," in terms of following God's creative intentions and attuning to the Mind of Christ.

Verses 6-11 highlight a basic difference between Jesus and some of his critics who were present. It is evident that the scribes did not relate forgiveness to a person's consciousness or inner life, but thought of it in other, less practical terms. They were thinking in their hearts: "Only God can forgive sin. Therefore, it is blasphemy to declare that a man's sins are forgiven." Believing in an angry God, they probably thought that God had cursed this young man because of his sins. What would have been the result if their attitude had prevailed? The young man would have remained lame and miserable, crippled emotionally and physically by his own hate. Jesus, in contrast, understood that Divine Love is always ready, willing, and able to heal. When the patient let go of his guilt, the power of God was released to do its perfect work.

Jesus declared, "The Son of man has authority (again, *exousia*) on Earth to forgive sins." (2:10) We are not concerned here with how the later Church, including even the gospel writers, understood the term "Son of man." What concerns us is how Jesus used it on this particular occasion. In the Aramaic language, which was his native tongue, "son of man" means a human being, as contrasted to an angel or an animal. Whether he made this statement in Aramaic or in Greek, the meaning is clear: Through an inner attunement with the Presence and Power of God, we are all empowered by grace to forgive ourselves and others. *When we understand this, we can no longer evade or overlook our essential function in forgiveness.* "Forgive us our debts, As we also have forgiven our debtors." (Matthew 6:12)

The scribes' claim that "only God can forgive" was thus, to use the vernacular, a cop-out. It is *people*, not God, who need to let go of what is false and degrading. The word translated "forgive" in our text (*aphiemi*) is based on a verb meaning "to let a ship loose from its moorings." In a more general sense, it means "to let go, to release, to permit to depart." It is true that Divine Love is the enabling power by which we practice forgiveness. In another sense, however, God does not forgive because He has never condemned.

Faith was necessary for the man's healing, as well as forgiveness. Of the patient and his four companions, it is said that "Jesus saw their faith." Yet faith alone did not bring a cure, nor is it the only factor in restoring wholeness. Some people seek healing consciously, but resist it subconsciously. There are others, including even an occasional atheist, who resist it consciously, but receive it subconsciously. Such split mentalities are not uncommon; thus, it is not unheard of for a nonbeliever to be healed while a devout person is not. Unless the group of five had a degree of faith, however, they would not have sought help at all. Certainly the paralytic's friends would not have made a

31

hole in the roof.

We are not favorable to would-be "faith healers" who try to place the full burden of cure on their clients' own faith, and then blame them if the healing does not occur.

Hebrews 11:1-3, when correctly understood, tells us a good deal about the true nature of faith: "Now faith is the assurance [*hypostasis*, "substance, reality, exact representation"] of things hoped for, the conviction [*elenchos*, "proof of ultimate realities"] of things not seen. For by it, the men of old received divine approval. By faith, we understand that the world was created by the word of God, so that what is seen was made out of things which do not appear." The New English Bible translates Hebrews 11:3 in a more direct way: "By faith, we perceive that the universe was fashioned by the word of God, so that the visible came forth from the invisible." Yes, the visible comes forth from the invisible, and faith *as Jesus understood it* provides insight into the invisible where prayers are *already* answered. Also, through us the invisible unfolds into visibility in a practical sense. The universal, creative law works in and through our consciousness, unfolding God's blessings which enter our everyday lives. One of these blessings is health.

It is well to affirm:

I HAVE FAITH IN THE ONE PRESENCE AND ONE POWER, GOD THE GOOD, ALL-GOVERNING.

THEREFORE, I HAVE FAITH IN MYSELF AS GOD'S IDEA. I HAVE FAITH IN MY ABILITY TO EXPRESS MY GOD-GIVEN CAPACITIES.

THE FAITH OF THE HEALING CHRIST IS NOW QUICKENED IN ME. I SEE BEYOND OUTER APPEARANCES, TO THE FULLNESS OF THE DIVINE PRESENCE. I AM HEALED.

Along with faith, the paralytic was restored because he let go of guilt, and forgave himself and others. Forgiving, in real terms, means casting out a certain type of negative thought or image, and filling the "vacant space" with positive thoughts and images; usually the opposite of the negative ones. We root out errors not by sugar-coating them, but by recognizing them first, and then confronting them with affirmative prayer.

Moving beyond guilt and into grace, then, involves three basic steps:
(1) Frankly and honestly recognize the nature of the problem (hate, resentment, seeing evil, etc.). We don't heal anything by "stuffing it," as the expression goes.
(2) Let go of the problem, mentally and emotionally. Though it has existed as a temporary fact (as it did for the paralytic), it has no basis in God's Mind or intentions, or in God's idea of ourselves, which is necessarily God-like.
(3) Use affirmative words, and hold positive visual images in mind, which are the opposite of the problem (love, blessing, seeing the good, etc.).

Note that there are no short-cuts; these steps must all be taken and in the order listed. First acknowledge the problem, then let go of it emotionally, and then use affirmative prayer and positive imagery. If you begin by using affirmations, without taking the first two steps, you are very likely to drive guilt feelings into the subconscious mind. Instead of cleansing the subconscious, you will create a greater negative reaction than before.

Modern neuroscience can add clarity on this point. That is to say, *there are two distinct ways of using language.* One is centered in the left brain hemisphere in most people, and functions in a logical, analytical way. Applied to theology, an example would be reciting a creed or doctrinal statement. The other involves the right hemisphere in a major way. It accepts lyrical and poetic imagery, is accompanied by mental picturing, and is sung or chanted. In most individuals, the left "specializes" in verbal and mathematical symbols, the right in visual symbols.

Affirmations, whether used by the individual or in a group, are used effectively in what is called a right-hemispheric mode of consciousness. For the "r-mode" is the doorway to the subconscious phase of mind. As an example, consider the statement: I AM ONE WITH GOD'S GOOD. THROUGH HIS POWER, MY LIFE IS BLESSED WITH ORDER AND PEACE. If repeated slowly and rhythmically, it can be used with great effect. It will tend to change the subconscious level at depth, expanding an awareness of the Divine Presence, and releasing greater peace and harmony into our lives. On the other hand, if we use it improperly to screen disorderly and warring elements out of awareness, we will succeed only in repressing our difficulties. As already noted, discord will reassert itself later with greater force.

Before the young man's healing, his leg muscles would have atrophied from not being used. It was thus important for him to get up and start walking, and to do it now. He would have been weak at first, but his muscles would have soon gained strength. There is a lesson here for us today: We need to take positive action in line with our faith. Though confidence leads to positive action, it works the other way, too; positive action reinforces confidence.

Finally, note that no person, humanly speaking, needs to stand alone, If there is a spiritually supportive prayer group in your area, join it. If there isn't, you can start your own affirmative prayer group. A good share of Jesus' healing work was done in the company of expectant people. As we read in Mark 2:2, "many were gathered together, so that there was no longer room for them, even about the door." Be assured that *collective* acceptance of Divine healing leads inevitably to more and greater healings.

Jesus had the ability to lead a group into common attunement with the Healing Christ. A single individual, in tune with God, can achieve much. A group united in thought and purpose, however, will be many times more effective. "If two of you agree on earth about anything they ask, it will be done for them by my Father in heaven. For where two or three are gathered in my name, there am I in the midst of them." (Matthew 18:19-20)

Chapter 5

Sick Man at Pool of Bethzatha

2Now there is in Jerusalem by the Sheep Gate a pool, in Hebrew called Bethzatha, which has five porticoes. 3In these lay a multitude of invalids, blind, lame, paralyzed. [Footnote: 3b-4--waiting for the moving of the water; for an angel of the Lord went down at certain seasons into the pool, and troubled the water; whoever stepped in first after the troubling of the water was healed of whatever disease he had.] 5One man was there, who had been ill for thirty-eight years. 6When Jesus saw him and knew that he had been lying there a long time, he said to him, "Do you want to be healed?" 7The sick man answered him, "Sir, I have no man to put me into the pool when the water is troubled, and while I am going, another steps down before me." 8Jesus said to him, "Rise, take up your pallet, and walk." 9And at once the man was healed, and he took up his pallet and walked. Now the day was the Sabbath. 10So the Jews said to the man who was cured, "It is the Sabbath, it is not lawful for you to carry your pallet." 11But he answered them, "The man who healed me said to me, 'Take up your pallet, and walk.'" 12They asked him, "Who is the man who said to you, 'Take up your pallet, and walk'?" 13Now the man who had been healed did not know who it was, for Jesus had withdrawn, as there was a crowd in the place. 14Afterward, Jesus found him in the temple, and said to him, "See, you are well! Sin no more, that nothing worse befall you."
–John 5:2-14

The narrative begins with a pathetic picture. Archaeologists have found the ruins of an actual pool with five porticoes in Jerusalem. In these five porches, "lay a multitude of invalids, blind, lame, paralyzed." This is a way of saying: Do not limit your vision to the five physical senses. God's ideas are infinite and are also within us. Thus, unlimited resources are available to heal, harmonize, and adjust the consciousness, body, and outer conditions of our lives. To identify with the omnipresent, harmonizing power of God, brings forth wholeness. To identify with a weak heart, a tumor, or a slipped disk, blocks the healing flow.

As stated in the last chapter, it can be a great help to join a prayer and meditation group. More of them are forming all the time. Churches sponsor many of them, and this is most encouraging; but many others spring directly from the felt needs of the people involved. They meet largely in private homes, and are a major factor in revitalizing the spiritual lives of people today.

Not all of these groups, however, have been effective. In some groups, though the members sincerely want healing to occur, they have a variety of beliefs about obstacles to healing. Quite apart from their pure and honest intentions, their imagery is negative and limiting, so that they actually give energy to the symptoms of people on their prayer lists. For example, a member might say, "Let's pray for Sam Jones. He has a very bad heart, and looked terrible the last time I saw him." It has happened more than once that when a person was thus prayed for, his conditioned worsened. On the other hand, his condition improved when the group ceased their prayers for him.

Affirm:

THE INFINITE PRESENCE THAT CALLED THE UNIVERSE INTO BEING, NOW FLOWS THROUGH ME.

THIS SAME PRESENCE INDWELLS, SUSTAINS, AND NOURISHES ME IN MIND, BODY, AND THE AFFAIRS OF EVERYDAY LIFE.

I PICTURE HEALTH, HARMONY, AND SUCCESS AT ALL TIMES.

The pool of water is both literal and figurative. It was an actual pool, and it also symbolizes the unhealed subconscious mind. The angel stirring the water, though a later addition to the text, represents Divine ideas penetrating the subconscious mind and bringing healing. Also, while the scribal note (3b-4) fails to interpret events accurately, it does reflect what many people believed at the time. John 5:7, which was part of the original text, refers indirectly to the popular belief about the angels at this pool.

Jesus asked the lame man if he wanted to be well; the older translation, "whole," says more and is still to be preferred. Wholeness is more than the absence of lameness. *Its true basis, and very essence, are found in the Healing Christ, the Universal Word or Logos that is the heart of all reality.* Only in a derived sense is wholeness mental, emotional, physical, and social. A state of consciousness attuned to the Eternal Word is what lifts our attention above the difficulty, and heals it.

Effective prayer groups give their attention to our status in the Mind of God. We grow in awareness as we behold and affirm the Christ in one another, and in ourselves. It is in the Christ that we find our essential, ontological oneness and, paradoxically, the basis for our individuality. It is in the Christ that the potential exists to heal the outer form.

Today, as in the First Century A.D., many people give lip service to God's power, but relatively few (though, happily, the number is growing steadily) realize that God is present and at work here and now. To many in ancient times, God had become like an old man who had once been in charge but who–to use a modern expression–had been "kicked upstairs," with the real power exercised by celestial beings of one kind or another. Jesus, however, cut through the sophistry and dualism of his era by calling God *Abba*, the informal Aramaic word meaning "Daddy." This was a way of saying that God is real, and loves and cares for us here and now. Paul caught the same basic vision when he contrasted the spirit of slavery with the spirit of sonship. Repeat Romans 8:14-17a often:

"ALL WHO ARE LED BY THE SPIRIT OF GOD ARE SONS OF GOD. FOR YOU DID NOT RECEIVE THE SPIRIT OF SLAVERY TO FALL BACK INTO FEAR, BUT YOU HAVE RECEIVED THE SPIRIT OF SONSHIP. WHEN WE CRY, 'ABBA! FATHER!' IT IS THE SPIRIT HIMSELF BEARING WITNESS WITH OUR SPIRIT THAT WE ARE CHILDREN OF GOD, AND IF CHILDREN, THEN HEIRS, HEIRS OF GOD AND FELLOW HEIRS WITH CHRIST."

Also, in your prayer group, use affirmations such as these written by H. B. Jeffery:

IN MY INTEGRITY WITHIN ME, WHERE I KNOW AND SEE AS GOD SEES, I KNOW AND SEE YOU, O BELOVED, TO BE FREE, WISE, IMMORTAL.

I SEE YOU TO BE THE STRONG SON OF GOD, BROTHER OF JESUS CHRIST AND JOINT HEIR OF THE FATHER TO THE KINGDOM. (Change the gender, if appropriate.)

I SEE YOU ALIVE WITH GOD AND UPHELD BY HIS FREE SPIRIT FOREVER.

The details are lost, but we have to wonder how any human being could stand the boredom of sitting by the side of a pool every day for 38 years, doing nothing. We can reasonably conclude that he had severe emotional problems of some kind. Jesus, of course, did not focus on pathology and illness, but on what would release the healing action of God. Again, to focus on the Presence and Power of God aligns our consciousness with the divine reality of health, and releases it into fuller expression.

"Wilt thou be made whole?" is a question we need to ask ourselves. It is natural to want to feel well and be well, but there must have been some kind of "pay-off" for being ill or incapacitated. People who have a positive motivation toward life either are healed, or make progress despite being ill or disabled, and either is a move toward wholeness. Doing nothing and feeling sorry for oneself is a move away from wholeness. Somehow, Jesus helped the man overcome his own resistance to being healed.

The man at the pool had forgotten that God was the *Source* of his health, no matter what the philosophy or method of treatment may be. He became dependent upon a particular method of healing, and a bizarre one at that, i.e., getting into a pool after the water became agitated, and then only before anyone else got in.

Jesus did not wait around until the water stirred again, for the man did not need to get into the water. His instructions were, "Rise, take up your pallet, and walk." And he did! This meant more than rising physically. He was to rise in consciousness to the fact that he was whole in God's sight, and to accept his life as a capable and responsible member of society.

When Jesus came, the sick recovered, the lame walked, the deaf heard, and the blind had their sight restored. The Healing

Christ is within you now as your eternal Identity, and is greater than any limiting factor in your soul or body. As I John 4:4 declares, "He who is in you is greater than he who is in the world." The Christ Idea of you is greater than your current self-image, and can progressively replace whatever is false or limiting with Its own truth, which is unlimited in resources.

Declare often:
I AFFIRM THE LOVE THAT GOD IS. GOD IS LOVE, AND I AM HIS CHILD. THEREFORE, MY DIVINE INHERITANCE IS NOT DISEASE OR FAILURE. AS AN HEIR OF GOD AND A FELLOW-HEIR WITH CHRIST, I AM HEALTHY, JOYFUL, AND CAPABLE. I CLAIM MY INHERITANCE NOW.

Tremendous energies are sometimes released through positive prayer. What is needed when that happens, is to give God the glory and live with confidence. There is, however, such a thing as over-confidence. People who have been emotionally crippled, as the man at the pool, need to *continue* to work at establishing positive habits and images, to replace the negative ones that brought them to ruin in the past. What did he need to do? Rebuke negative mental pictures, and replace them with positive ones. And do anything positive, whether it be to work at a craft, tend a garden, paint a picture, or otherwise work creatively with his hands.

Again, if you find yourself in a situation of this kind, you do not need to stand alone, humanly speaking. Join a positive, faith-filled group whose members are oriented in their thinking to the love and goodness of God. Avoid groups that teach an angry or condemning God. What you need is an uplifting environment that will help provide *a way out* of the negative pattern that once dominated your beliefs about yourself, other people, and life in general.

John 5:14 states: "Afterward, Jesus found him in the temple, and said to him, 'See, you are well! Sin [miss the mark] no more, that nothing worse befall you.'" This was a stern warning–exactly what he needed to hear–not to resume negative habits of thought and action. If he resumed the ways that led to his previous incapacity, he would create a more severe difficulty for himself than before.

Here are some affirmations that will be helpful:

I AM AN ILLUMINED CHILD OF GOD, FILLED WITH THE SPIRIT OF DIVINE LOVE AND WISDOM, BY WHICH I AM GUIDED IN ALL MY WAYS, AND LED INTO THAT WHICH IS FOR MY HIGHEST GOOD.

THROUGH THE SPIRIT OF GOD IN ME, I AM PROGRESSIVELY HEALED TO THE DEPTHS OF MY SOUL. I AM DIVINELY GUIDED IN WAYS THAT ARE FOR MY HIGHEST GOOD, AND THE HIGHEST GOOD OF OTHERS.

I GO FORWARD WITH CONFIDENCE AND STRENGTH. WITH THE LOVE OF GOD INSPIRING ME, ALL THINGS WORK TOGETHER FOR GOOD.

As Jesus assures us, "You will know the truth, and the truth will make you free." (John 8:32)

Chapter 6

The Man with a Withered Hand

6On another sabbath, when he entered the synagogue and taught, a man was there whose right hand was withered. 7And the scribes and the Pharisees watched him, to see whether he would heal on the sabbath, so that they might find an accusation against him. 8But he knew their thoughts, and he said to the man who had the withered hand, "Come and stand here." And he rose and stood there. 9And Jesus said to them, "I ask you, is it lawful on the sabbath to do good or to do harm, to save life or to destroy it?" 10And he looked around on them all, and said to them, "Stretch out your hand." And he did so, and his hand was restored. 11But they were filled with fury and discussed with one another what they might do to Jesus.
–Luke 6:6-11 (parallel passages: Matthew 12:9-14; Mark 3:1-6)

Jerome (340-420), a Christian scholar of late antiquity, recorded an excerpt from the lost *Gospel According to the Hebrews*. Since this fragment fits well with the Biblical record, its information is probably correct. It states that the man told Jesus:

> "I was a mason, seeking a living with my hands; I beg you, Jesus, restore my health to me, so that I need not beg for my food in shame."**1**

According to Jerome's information, then, the man came to Jesus begging for help. Still, he had much in his favor. As far as we can tell, he was completely willing to be healed, and had no mixed motives in this respect. In fact, he had a strong motive *for* recovery. This was to resume his trade as a stone mason, a craft which requires strength and the full use of one's hands.

With Jerome's data added, we find a vital clue. Note the dramatic contrast between the begging attitude of the patient and the stance of the Great Physician. The basic problem was spiritual, namely the man's belief in his own inadequacy. He did not trust the deeper levels of his own being to lead him in ways of health, confidence, and all around well-being. Jesus, by contrast, told him, in effect, that he was already whole and perfect in God's sight. When conscious of the Divine Presence, we are awake to our true being as whole, undivided, and one with the cosmos. What the man needed to do was to relax and accept this truth for himself.

This healing occurred on the sabbath. Setting aside one day in seven for worship and rest is certainly one of God's ideas. In the Biblical allegory of creation, we read: "On the seventh day God finished his work which he had done, and he rested on the seventh day from all his work which he had done. So God blessed the seventh day and hallowed it, because on it God rested from all his work which he had done in creation." (Genesis 2:2-3)

There is a deeper meaning here, however, than formal worship and ceasing work. The Sabbath, in a spiritual sense, is inner peace and rest in communion with God. Malinda E. Cramer, Divine Science founder (1844-1906), wrote eloquently on this subject:

"To keep the Sabbath Day holy, is to remember wholeness; which, to do, is to cease laboring to be, and striving to exist, and be and do what we see the Father doing, that it may be understandingly said that it is God who doeth the works in all living. Has not His mind made all these things? Is not creation an image of His mind? Let us then cease laboring to perfect His works, and accept them in their perfection, and rest; for in oneness of consciousness, there is no strife, no sin, no discord. Unity, strength, peace, plenty, is the state or condition of One."**2**

Wholeness is divinely natural, the law of our being. Accordingly, Jesus had to persuade the stone mason to stop struggling and straining for what was already his in the sight of God. Once he entered the consciousness of the spiritual sabbath, the physical adjustment would follow. This does not mean that he needed to *try* to be perfect, or to *attain* an unrealized spiritual state. He needed to relax and, as we say, "let go and let God."

The scene of the healing shows that Jesus had strong opposition from a group of scribes and Pharisees on this occasion. Jesus made a devastating argument based on a contrast between his own motives and those of his critics. He declared, "I ask you, is it lawful on the sabbath to do good or to do harm, to save life or to destroy it?" (Luke 6:9) He implied that in their own twisted view, it was "lawful" *to plot his destruction* on the Sabbath, yet it was sacrilege for him *to heal* on the sabbath! "But they were silent." (Mark 3:4) He had bared the total absurdity of their position.

Indeed, the situation was the opposite of what it appeared superficially to be. The sabbath, in its deeper sense, is an inward state of ease and rest, grounded in conscious oneness with God and the cosmos. Jesus released healing on the sabbath (as at all other times) through an inner realization of ease and rest. This violated the letter of the law, but upheld its spirit. Unknown to themselves, the scribes and Pharisees were the actual sabbath breakers, not Jesus, and they showed it by their attitudes and actions.

That Jesus' opponents had serious designs against him is seen by the Greek word translated "accusation" [*kategoria*] in

Luke 6:7. It meant a criminal charge in a court of law. According to Roman law, magic was outlawed, and some people were convicted of practicing magic. The scribes and Pharisees in question could have had Jesus indicted either under Roman law as a magician, or before the Sanhedrin (the authoritative council of Jewish elders in Jerusalem) as a sabbath breaker. On this occasion, they probably considered a Roman trial. "The Pharisees went out and immediately held counsel with the Herodians against him, how to destroy him." (Mark 3:6) Herod Antipas, a son of Herod the Great, ruled Galilee at the time. They probably talked to members of his court about making formal charges.

To convict Jesus as a magician, however, they would have needed tangible evidence such as scrolls containing magic spells, amulets, talismans, and the like. There is no evidence that Jesus ever used or possessed such scrolls or devices.

"And he looked around on them all." (Luke 6:10) Jesus not only silenced his critics, but he was able to gather the mental focus of the people who were present. When we gather the mental focus in this way, we also multiply the active energy to get things done. In so doing, he also increased the expectancy of the synagogue's members as to what was about to occur. Without doubt, this contributed to the positive outcome.

Also, when Jesus told the man with the withered hand to "Come and stand here [*egeire kai stethi eis to meson*]," he meant more than the translation shows. He involved the patient spiritually and mentally, as well as physically. The wording of the Greek text actually means, "Be awakening and standing into the midst." That is, stand up in the realization that you are already one with the resources of God's kingdom–indeed, one with God who has healed you.

In the spirit of Jesus' words, affirm:

I AWAKE FROM ILLUSION TO REALITY.

I RISE FROM ERROR INTO TRUTH.

I ACCEPT THAT IN SPIRIT AND IN TRUTH, I AM ALREADY HEALED.

You may have personal shortcomings that seem very real and pressing. Remember, though, you need not *try* to be perfect. "Trying" is not what it's about. The concept of co-creation, mentioned in the Introduction to this book, is a valid and far-reaching one. It does, however, have its limits. To claim healing, we have to free ourselves from the arrogant folly of trying to create truth, or wholeness, out of nothing. (God unfolds creation out of Himself. Contrary to many theologians, even God does not create something out of nothing.) In the case of this patient, the turning point toward healing was probably the cessation of strained effort.

Jesus' second command to him, "Stretch out your hand," shows his complete confidence that the healing was done. Jesus did not beg; he accepted. More than a physical healing occurred. At the same time, he restored the man's confidence in his own worth and in the Divine Source of life.

Paul noted, "There are celestial bodies and there are terrestial bodies; but the glory of the celestial is one, and the glory of the terrestial is another." (I Corinthians 15:40) The celestial or etheric body is a present fact of our being; it survives physical death. It also provides the pattern or template from which the terrestial (earth) body forms, grows, and is sustained and maintained, from the inside out. The etheric body is never deformed or disabled, but provides the vehicle through which the

Divine Word, the I AM or Christ, becomes flesh in us and as us. If we consider only the physical body, we lose sight of the unity of Spirit-soul-body, and of the unlimited nature of the cosmos which indwells us. The Healing Christ ever seeks a fuller and freer expression through us as health, harmony, and strength.

A key point–which calls for clear understanding, not mere lip service–is that we are not human beings trying to be spiritual. We are spiritual beings having a human experience, progressively awakening to our true inheritance of oneness with God.

Declare, calmly and confidently:

THE CLEANSING, HEALING, VITALIZING ACTION OF THE INDWELLING CHRIST NOW MAKES ME WHOLE AND FREE.

Many people are mentally and physically sick because they are in a chronic state of tension. God, other people, and the Earth itself are interpreted as threats to their well-being. Above all, they do not trust themselves. There is, however, a way out of this pathetic and unnatural state. Relaxation, meditation, deep breathing, and a shift in one's trend of thought and imagery are basic steps toward recovering one's innate confidence and sense of peace. This is more important than bodily healing, though that often follows, too.

One way to relax is to tell various parts of the body to relax. Before doing so, take a few deep breaths. Then begin with the top of your head, and work downward toward your toes. Keep your eyes closed while doing this. For example, say to your hands, "IN THE NAME OF THE HEALING CHRIST, RELAX, RELAX, RELAX, LET GO, LET GOD."

Then, having completed this relaxation exercise, affirm:

THERE IS ONLY ONE PRESENCE AND ONE POWER IN THE UNIVERSE, GOD THE GOOD, ALL-GOVERNING. I AM SAFE AND SECURE IN HIS PRESENCE.

GOD LOVES AND ACCEPTS ME NOW. THEREFORE, I ACCEPT MY HEALING NOW. I RELAX, LET GO, AND LET GOD.

Of course, in healing work, not only the individual, but also the group situation, should be considered. If you want to be a healing channel in the presence of a group, be sure to prepare a favorable mental atmosphere. Eliminate or minimize the influence of scoffers. Also, focus on the healing goal at hand, which includes involving favorable people on a spiritual level.

Luke 6:10 declares the outcome: "His hand was restored." The Greek verb translated "restored" [*apokathistemi*] actually means, "I set up again; I restore to its original condition." The term, as used in this context, implies that a state of spiritual, mental, and physical harmony is our natural inheritance. This innate pattern of wholeness is implanted in our etheric bodies, and can in turn become implanted in every cell of our Earth bodies, and even change DNA where needed. The sense of the Greek verb dovetails exactly with the spiritual sabbath as discussed above. Rejoice, therefore, that Divine Order is real, and is the real of you.

Chapter 7

Healing at a Distance

2Now a centurion had a slave who was dear to him, who was sick and at the point of death. 3When he heard of Jesus, he sent to him elders of the Jews, asking him to come and heal his slave. 4And when they came to Jesus, they besought him earnestly, saying, "He is worthy to have you do this for him, 5for he loves our nation, and he built us our synagogue." 6And Jesus went with them. When he was not far from the house, the centurion sent friends to him, saying to him, "Lord, do not trouble yourself, for I am not worthy to have you come under my roof; 7therefore, I did not presume to come to you. But say the word, and let my servant be healed. 8For I am a man set under authority, with soldiers under me: and I say to one, 'Go,' and he goes; and to another, 'Come,' and he comes; and to my slave, 'Do this,' and he does it." 9When Jesus heard this, he marveled at him, and turned and said to the multitude that followed him, "I tell you, not even in Israel have I found such faith." 10And when those who had been sent returned to the house, they found the slave well.

–Luke 7:2-10 (parallel passage: Matthew 8:5-13)

The two accounts we will review in this chapter would seem impossible to a materialist. Yet, as Dr. Dossey points out, so-called remote healing is a fact of life, verified by experimental evidence.

When we look to God for healing, it is valid at the same time to seek the help of a prayer ministry in attuning ourselves with

God's healing Presence. If you seek such help, you will find people who have various degrees of contact with the public. Some counselors prefer to work directly with individuals and families. They make hospital calls, not merely to visit, but with a serious healing purpose. They also make home calls upon request.

Others conduct meetings, often large ones, to which the general public is invited. This has the advantage of tapping vast reserves of psychic energy for a healing purpose. The disadvantage is the general lack of continuity and follow-up. Many people receive immediate help, and sometime the results are permanent. Relapses occur, however, in the cases of those who do not change the negative belief system that produced the discordant condition in the first place.

Still others work in organized healing groups, but offer little direct counseling. People contact them for prayer help by letter, phone, or e-mail. Then the group sends them a letter and an affirmative prayer statement, and continues praying with them for a set period, usually 30 days.

All these approaches are useful, and it is interesting to observe *that Jesus was effective with all three*. He worked successfully with some people privately, with others in the presence of large groups, and with still others at a distance without any physical contact. He typically obtained the active cooperation of those needing help, but not in every case.

Jesus as a person, even in his resurrected and ascended state, cannot be everywhere at once. The Healing Christ, however, is All-in-all, fully present everywhere in the Omnipresence of God. When we are attuned to Omnipresence, we release Its harmonizing action wherever the point of need may be. Limits such as "here" or "there," "then" and "now," are as irrelevant to

God as they are to the Internet. Also, in prayer work we are *not* dealing with any wave length of electromagnetic energy. The results of prayer do not diminish with the square of the distance, as applies, for example, to sound vibrations.

The essential in Divine healing is an inward realization of oneness with God, which includes oneness with whomever we are including in prayer. God's Love moves through us in a conscious way. We begin with faith, but the seeds of expanding awareness are inherent within this faith. It is so simple, in essence, that we must be alert not to lose sight of its simplicity. Affirm:

WHEREVER I AM, GOD IS IN ALL HIS FULLNESS. I AM CONSCIOUS OF THE UNIVERSAL HARMONY IN WHICH I LIVE, MOVE, AND HAVE MY BEING.

WHEREVER I AM, GOD IS PRESENT AS PERFECT HEALTH. THE HEALING, HARMONIZING, VITALIZING PRESENCE OF GOD NOW RENEWS MY MIND AND BODY.

WHEREVER I AM, GOD IS PRESENT AS PERFECT WISDOM. THROUGH THE STILL, SMALL VOICE WITHIN, I AM LED INTO MY HIGHEST GOOD.

WHEREVER I AM, GOD IS PRESENT AS PERFECT SUPPLY. I AM GUIDED IN NEW WAYS TO SUCCESS AND PROSPERITY.

The key issue in the healing of the centurion's servant is *faith*, and how faith gets things done in practical terms. "Not even in Israel have I found such faith." (Luke 7:9) As Jesus practiced it, however, faith is not a form of naive belief. Nor is it a system of doctrines, such as "The Christian Faith." Rather, it involves active confidence and trust, inspired from within as we open ourselves to the love and wisdom of the Christ. Faith, as Jesus used and understood it, relates directly to the activation of spiritual power and authority to meet human needs, here and now. The more we *expect* spiritual law to work through us, the more the law is channeled to produce positive outcomes. This is inherent in the law itself. Active faith releases definite results, especially when linked to the imaging power of the mind.

The Greek word for trust appears both as a noun [*pistis*] and as a verb [*pisteuo*] in the New Testament. Generally, the noun is translated "faith," and the verbal form is rendered "believe." This has led to a serious misunderstanding in which people tend to equate faith with blind belief. Belief, however, is only one of several aspects of what we call faith. The Greek words that the text uses both derive from an ancient verb [*peitho*] which meant "to rely by inward certainty, to agree, to have confidence, to obey, to yield, to trust." A person could conceivably *believe* anything. *Faith*, however, is an inner assurance that God is in charge of a situation; a quiet trust that things will therefore work out for good; a way of seeing past appearances to the wholeness of the Divine Presence.

The centurion, a Roman military officer, showed a true understanding of faith. He compared the lawful, delegated authority he had over his soldiers to the authority that Jesus exercised over disease, disability, and other outer conditions.1 He expected, and took for granted, that his men would obey his orders. By analogy, his appeal to Jesus was: If you speak the word for healing, my slave (or "my boy," if translated from the Aramaic in the Gospel of Matthew) will be healed. Jesus fully agreed, and commended the centurion for his understanding of faith. "And when those who had been sent returned to the house, they found the slave well." (Luke 7:10)

The healing of the official's son also occurred "at a distance." Some scholars have concluded that the two healings actually go back to a single event. Given the differences in detail, this is unlikely. The basic pattern is the same, however, and is apparent in both events. The account reads as follows:

46So he came again to Cana in Galilee, where he had made the water wine. And at Capernaum there was an official whose son was ill. 47When he heard that Jesus had come from Judea to Galilee, he went and begged him to come down and heal his son, for he was at the point of death. 48Jesus therefore said to him, "Unless you see signs and wonders, you will not believe." 49The official said to him, "Sir, come down before my child dies." 50Jesus said to him, "Go; your son will live." The man believed the word that Jesus spoke to him and went his way. 51As he was going down, his servants met him and told him that his son was living. 52So he asked them the hour when he began to mend, and they said to him, "Yesterday at the seventh hour the fever left him." 53The father knew that was the hour when Jesus had said to him, "Your son will live"; and he himself believed, and all his household. 54This was now the second sign that Jesus did when he had come from Judea to Galilee.
–John 4:46-54

It is significant that in the Gospel of John, the Greek word for faith never appears as a noun, but always, and frequently, as a verb. The emphasis is on *action*, an inner quickening followed by tangible results.

The official who came seeking help for his son had a challenge of faith, unlike the centurion. At first, he apparently thought that Jesus would have to physically touch his child in order to heal him. In the course of the conversation, however–the details of which are lost to us–he became convinced that distance didn't matter. To some degree at least, the father experienced an inner awakening, an expansion of awareness that made him less bound by outer appearances.

As in most other cases, Jesus gave the person seeking help something *specific* to do, as an expression of trust: "Jesus said to him, 'Go; your son will live.' The man believed the word that Jesus spoke to him and went his way." (John 4:50) Later, the man's servants met him on the way home, and verified that the crisis had passed at the time that Jesus said, "your son will live."

It is quite common for healers to know when their affirmative prayers have been effective. This is a kind of intuition, and does not need to be explained in order to function. It was no different two millennia ago. For example, *The Babylonian Talmud*, Berakoth 34b reads:

> Once a son of Rabban Gamaliel (II) was ill. He sent two disciples to R. Hanina b. Dosa, that he might pray for mercy for him. When he (b. Dosa) saw them, he went up into the attic and implored mercy for him. When he came down he said to them, "Go, for the fever has left him." They said to him, "Are you a prophet then?" He answered them, "I am no prophet, nor am I a prophet's son; but thus I have received tradition: When my prayer runs freely in my mouth, I know that the person concerned has been accepted; but if it does not, I know that he will be carried off." They returned and noted the hour in writing. When they came back to Rabban Gamaliel he said to them, "By the temple service! You have said neither too little nor too much; it happened exactly so that in that hour the fever left him and he asked for water to drink."[2]

Remote healing can be a fact of *your* experience. Remember that in the Healing Christ, the only place is here and the only time is now. We do not rely on personal skill or achievement, but on the Presence and Power of God within us.

Affirm:

I HAVE FAITH IN THE PRESENCE AND POWER OF GOD, MIGHTY IN THE MIDST OF ME TO ACCOMPLISH ALL THINGS.

I HAVE FAITH IN THE INDWELLING SPIRIT OF GOD NOW RENEWING AND HEALING MY MIND AND BODY.

I HAVE FAITH IN THE INDWELLING SPIRIT OF GOD NOW INSPIRING ME WITH ITS TRUTH, AND GUIDING ME IN ALL MY WAYS.

I HAVE FAITH IN THE INDWELLING SPIRIT OF GOD NOW MANIFESTING AS ABUNDANCE IN ALL MY AFFAIRS.

Chapter 8

The Swine Miracle

1They came to the other side of the sea, to the country of the Gerasenes. 2And when he had come out of the boat, there met him out of the tombs a man with an unclean spirit, 3who lived among the tombs; and no one could bind him any more, even with a chain; 4for he had often been bound with fetters and chains, but the chains he wrenched apart, and the fetters he broke in pieces; and no one had the strength to subdue him. 5Night and day among the tombs and on the mountains he was always crying out, and bruising himself with stones. 6And when he saw Jesus from afar, he ran and worshiped him; 7and crying out with a loud voice, he said, "What have you to do with me, Jesus, Son of the Most High God? I adjure you by God, do not torment me." 8For he had said to him, "Come out of the man, you unclean spirit!" 9And Jesus asked him, "What is your name?" He replied, "My name is Legion; for we are many." 10And he begged him eagerly not to send them out of the country. 11Now a great herd of swine was feeding there on the hillside; 12and they begged him, "Send us to the swine, let us enter them." 13So he gave them leave. And the unclean spirits came out, and entered the swine; and the herd, numbering about two thousand, rushed down the steep bank into the sea, and were drowned in the sea.

14The herdsmen fled, and told it in the city and in the country. And people came to see what it was that had happened. 15And they came to Jesus, and saw the demoniac sitting there, clothed and in his right mind, the man who had had the legion; and they were afraid. 16And those who had

seen it told what had happened to the demoniac and to the swine. **17**And they began to beg Jesus to depart from their neighborhood. **18**And as he was getting into the boat, the man who had been possessed with demons begged him that he might be with him. **19**But he refused, and said to him, "Go home to your friends, and tell them how much the Lord has done for you, and how he has had mercy on you." **20**And he went away and began to proclaim in the Decapolis how much Jesus had done for him; and all men marveled.
–Mark 5:1-20 (parallel passages: Matthew 8:28-34; Luke 8:26-39)

This story is so unlike our everyday lives that many readers don't take it seriously. They believe it only because it is in the Bible, or they don't believe it–period. It is apparent, however, that there is a solid core of fact behind the somewhat fanciful way of telling the story that we find here. It was an actual event, and the essentials of what happened can still be sorted out.

There is only one site that fits the geographic features, with the steep bank on the eastern shore of the Sea of Galilee. This is the village of Kursi or Khersa, which was located near the sea. In fact, the early Christians built a church–as a monument to the swine miracle–on site at Kursi. The ruins of the church are still there, so the location and the monument agree.

A mistake evidently occurred in translating the Aramaic oral tradition into Greek. The Gerasenes referred to in Mark 5:1 were the people of the city of Gerasa, located 35 miles to the southeast. Pigs today are not unlike those of 2000 years ago, and the pigs could not have run 35 miles at a stretch. They are basically sprinters, and they do not have the stamina to run long distances. Their limit is about half a mile.

The cemetery dweller's actions showed a completely demented state. He yelled and screamed constantly, and mutilated his own body with stones. Patients in mental hospitals who do this are drugged and put in strait-jackets, or otherwise restrained for their own protection.

There is no doubt, also, about the *public's* perception of the man's problem. They considered him to be demon-possessed, and he almost certainly believed it himself, playing the role that the public had laid on him. According to popular belief, demons dwelt in cemeteries, shrieked loudly, and often showed superhuman strength. In our account, the man lived in a cemetery. He had been shackled, probably hand and foot, but still could not be restrained. Also, people believed that when demons were immersed in water, they could not harm anyone. The pigs rushed over the bank and destroyed themselves.

His psychosis was obviously deep-seated. The modern label for this condition is *multiple personality disorder* (MPD). MPD can result from a child being severely abused, either physically or sexually. Or, it can result if important people in a child's life are assaulted and killed in his or her presence.

At one point, the man said, "My name is Legion; for we are many." (5:9) Leslie Weatherhead suggested that he may have had a bad experience with a Roman legion, and this is at least an educated guess. Perhaps as a child, he saw his parents, relatives, or friends killed or tortured during an insurrection against Roman rule. Such revolts did occur.

We need not conclude that anyone or anything entered the swine. The man's wild ravings would have been enough to stampede a restless herd of pigs, especially at night. The swineherds would have believed that the animals had been possessed. This was not only in keeping with the beliefs of the time, but would have prevented them from being blamed for the pigs' destruction.

In the Jewish system, pigs were ceremonially unclean and still are to this day. You will never find a pork chop in a kosher butcher shop. The owners of the herds would have noted that Jesus was a rabbi–albeit an unconventional one–and that 2000 animals had been destroyed. Already they had lost a major investment, and it is obvious that they considered Jesus to be a threat to their business. He, and not the swineherds, took the blame. The owners had reason to fear that many people would convert to Judaism, refuse to eat pork, and perhaps even destroy the remaining herds. Therefore, although greatly impressed by the healing, they did not wait long before asking him to leave.

The reader may wonder how such a healing could occur. It is clear that Jesus had to communicate with the patient's belief system before he could overturn it. This doesn't mean that the belief system in question made any sense, or that Jesus agreed with it. It means that there had to be a mental point of contact on some level, to penetrate through the patient's defenses.

We find, of course, that the man's frantic and threatening statements and gestures did not frighten Jesus. When threatened, the usual human reaction is one of two kinds: fight or flight. Jesus was so centered in the Divine Presence that he remained calm, and neither attacked nor fled. This kept him safe and enabled him to master the situation.

The man evidently made a practice of attacking people if they ventured near the cemetery. As he approached Jesus, however, his attitude changed from one of attack to that of respect. Jesus' consciousness of peace and nonresistance would have accomplished this. He did not, however, worship him as the translation indicates. Rather, he bowed before him in the Oriental fashion, as a way of paying him homage and showing respect.

How did Jesus work to communicate with the man's belief system? It is necessary here to point out that there are differences in grammatical structure between ancient Greek and modern English. *While the healing records in the gospels are short, they are made to appear even shorter in translation.* When Jesus declared, "come out of the man, you unclean spirit!" (Mark 5:8), the Greek verb is in the imperfect tense, implying continuing action. In the original text, therefore, Jesus made this statement not just once, but many times–repeatedly. Evidently the initial effort failed.

Jesus, however, shifted his tactics. Even if a patient is psychotic, if he yields a degree of trust, the healer has opened a channel through which spiritual power can and will flow. His new approach was to ask the man, "What is your name?" (5:9) And, as shown in the Greek text, he did so repeatedly. In the traditional Near East, there was great reluctance to making one's true name known. *A name was identified with power, so that if one knew someone's true name, he also gained control over him. A name also signified the nature and character of someone or something, as it does generally in the Bible.* When Jesus asked, "What is your name?", he would therefore have had a twofold purpose:

First, according to the prevailing belief system of that time and place, he would have gained actual control over the patient. The request of Jesus to be told his name was thus a request that the victim yield active trust to him. In so doing, the patient ceased to give power to whatever controlled him in his own psyche. This also opened the way for the healing action of God to take place in his consciousness.

Second, the man's difficulty was deeply buried on a subconscious level. Jesus wanted to lift it above the threshold of conscious mind, where it could be dealt with and then released. In effect, Jesus asked him, "What is the nature of the problem?"

His reply, "My name is Legion; for we are many." (Mark 5:9), shows that his psyche was split and dissociated in a number of directions. His past experiences had been so terrible that his central focus of awareness had disintegrated. Instead, a variety of sub-personalities held sway. The "Legion" served as a kind of collective voice representing these fragmentary personalities.

Once Jesus gained the man's confidence, the healing process began. He drew the underlying problem to the surface, and the man's reaction would have been wild and frenzied. This would have caused the pigs to stampede, and to rush headlong over the cliff and into the sea.

When the patient came to trust the Divine Presence at work through Jesus, the domination of what was discordant in him was weakened and finally dissolved. This resulted in a complete healing. "And they came to Jesus, and saw the demoniac sitting there, clothed and in his right mind." (Mark 5:15) Because he had found his true center in the Indwelling Christ, he had changed completely. The neighbors found him in his right mind, properly clothed, self-disciplined, and radiating a consciousness of God's peace.

As Jesus entered the boat and was about to leave, the healed man begged Jesus that he might also climb aboard and remain with him. (Mark 5:18) He refused, and instead told him to return to his friends and tell them what God (not Jesus on a personal level) had done for him. (Mark 5:19) This gave him a new mission and purpose. While he had once been obsessed with what was false and negative, he now directed his efforts to proclaiming the goodness and active power of God. (Mark 5:20) He served as a walking advertisement for Jesus' healing message. He also strengthened the positive direction of his own life by thus giving of himself to others.

There was, in all likelihood, a second motive for the refusal. Many people worship Jesus as God, but it is obvious that Jesus did *not* want to be worshiped or placed on a pedestal. If he did, he would have welcomed the healee aboard and received his worship, or at least his flattery. No, Jesus discouraged hero-worship. To the contrary, Jesus was determined that others would discover the Christ within themselves, as their own spiritual Identity. He wanted others to find their own divine Center, and to show forth its vitality, freedom, and power. To state the issue concisely, instead of allowing himself to be flattered by a new, hero-worshiping disciple, he led him into positive ways of thought and action that would secure permanent spiritual progress.

Affirm:

I, TOO, AM GOD'S PERFECT IDEA, THE CHRIST.

I DO NOT WORSHIP PERSONALITY. I AM ATTUNED TO THE ONE PRESENCE, ONE MIND, ONE POWER, IN WHOM I LIVE AND MOVE AND HAVE MY BEING.

Chapter 9

The Woman with an Issue of Blood

25There was a woman who had a flow of blood for twelve years, 26and who had suffered under many physicians, and had spent all that she had, and was no better, but rather grew worse. 27She had heard the reports about Jesus, and came up behind him in the crowd and touched his garment. 28For she said, "If I touch even his garments, I shall be made well." 29And immediately the hemorrhage ceased; and she felt in her body that she was healed of her disease. 30And Jesus, perceiving in himself that power had gone forth from him, immediately turned about in the crowd, and said, "Who touched my garments?" 31And his disciples said to him, "You see the crowed pressing around you, and yet you say, 'Who touched me?'" 32And he looked around to see who had done it. 33But the woman, knowing what had been done to her, came in fear and trembling and fell down before him, and told him the whole truth. 34And he said to her, "Daughter, your faith has made you well; go in peace, and be healed of your disease."
–Mark 5:25-34 (parallel passages: Matthew 9:20-22; Luke 8:43-48)

This account dramatically portrays the power of faith when linked with creative imagination. The woman was thoroughly convinced that if she touched Jesus' clothes, she would be made whole. Although sick, she mentally pictured herself well. Trust and expectancy, when linked with holding a mental picture, always change conditions in the body, and even in the larger environment. Touching Jesus' garment served as a point of contact which released the power of faith within her.

Rabbis wore a fringe or tassel, called a *zizith*, on their robes. According to the Gospels of Matthew and Luke–a detail missing from Mark, but probably authentic–this is what the woman touched. It reminded Jewish teachers that the Lord, I AM or Jahveh, is God and therefore has supreme power. The Presence of God still offers healing and deliverance, seeking to lift us all out of the "Egyptian bondage" of error and limitation.

Numbers 15:37-41 declares:

The Lord said to Moses, "Speak to the people of Israel, and bid them to make tassels on the corners of their garments throughout their generations, and to put upon the tassel of each corner a cord of blue; and it shall be to you a tassel to look upon and remember all the commandments of the Lord, to do them, not to follow after your own heart and your own eyes, which you are inclined to go after wantonly. So you shall remember and do all my commandments, and be holy to your God. I am the Lord your God, who brought you out of the land of Egypt, to be your God: I am the Lord your God."

Jesus took seriously those elements of the Scriptures that make a vital difference for all people everywhere, that deal with the human heart, that is to say, with people's spirituality and consciousness, including what modern psychologists recognize as subconscious. Like Ezekiel, he found the elders of Israel in his own times to be trapped in false chambers of imagery. (Ezekiel 8:12) And, like Jeremiah, he foresaw a new day when the nations would no longer walk after the imagination of their evil heart. (Jeremiah 3:17)

The failure of much prayer can be accounted for by the prayer focusing not on the Presence of God, but on the negative condition. Even if the words are positive and good, the images are negative and discordant. This is "to follow after your own heart and your own eyes, which you are inclined to go after wantonly." Yet by focusing on the Divine Presence, the I AM, and thus turning in word *and* imagery from the condition, we find the condition healed. In the Mind of God, like produces like. Our consciousness, when linked with the Mind of God, is opened to the whole universe of God's infinite ideas. This same consciousness is incarnated bodily; the wholeness of the cosmos is shown forth through the individual soul and body. This is true healing.

Returning to the case at hand, we can admire the woman's courage and determination. She had to push through crowds of people in order to reach Jesus. This must have been difficult in her weakened state. More than that, however, it was against the ceremonial laws of purity. We have noted that Jesus rejected these customs and ignored them in practice, but the woman probably didn't know that.

According to Leviticus 15:19-30, she was ceremonially unclean and also made everyone she touched, including Jesus, unclean. Leviticus 15:25 states: "If a woman has a discharge of blood for many days, not at the time of her impurity, or if she has a discharge beyond the time of her impurity, all the days of the discharge she shall continue in uncleanness; as in the days of her impurity, she shall be unclean."

To repeat, Jesus understood that cleanness and uncleanness have to do with the condition of one's mind and soul. (How we live and take care of ourselves is important, of course, but as an *expression* of our consciousness.) He stated specifically that *her* faith had made her whole. The older translation "whole" says more than "well," and should have been retained. *Being well*, according to popular belief, can carry the diminished meaning of the mere absence or removal of a discordant condition–of not being sick. Wholeness is a basic quality of God's Omnipresence, expressed outwardly as harmony, integrity, and balance. Also, a more adequate translation would relate that Jesus told the woman not merely to be made whole, but to enter into conscious wholeness as a *permanent* condition.**1** And, instead of "go in peace," a more accurate translation would have Jesus invite her to "enter into a *condition* of peace."**2** This would be a true condition of cleanness, as Jesus understood it.

To state the issue succinctly, Jesus did more than remove disease–he embraced wholeness with a full heart.

The account, then, implies a course of thought and action that anyone can take, with positive results. It tells us that "imagination" is *not* to be equated with "imaginary" in this context. The lesson is clear: *Never underestimate the energy released through creative imagery.* Visualize yourself as strong, healthy, and capable in mind, body, and action. Rebuke negative images, but do not fight them and thus give them more energy than they would otherwise have. Focus on what is good, true, and beautiful, and you will reap accordingly.

Affirm *and* visualize:

GOD IN THE MIDST OF ME IS MIGHTY TO HEAL. I SEE MYSELF AS GOD SEES ME, WHOLE, STRONG, AND WELL.

GOD IN THE MIDST OF ME IS MIGHTY TO GUIDE AND DIRECT. I SEE MYSELF AS GOD SEES ME, INTELLIGENT, WISE, AND UNDERSTANDING.

GOD IN THE MIDST OF ME IS MIGHTY TO BLESS AND PROSPER. I SEE MYSELF AS GOD SEES ME, CAPABLE AND ABUNDANTLY SUPPLIED.

There is a great advantage to using spiritual laws consciously. For then we can think and do what is positive, and avoid thinking and doing what is negative, on a consistent basis. If we "sow to the Spirit" and not to the negative appearance of things, we reap what is good and positive, not what is evil and corrupt. This is the same, in principle, as learning the difference between planting wheat and thistles. When our early ancestors began to farm, they learned to choose certain seeds to plant and to reject others. Today, we are learning the same selection process regarding the thoughts and images of the mind. The potential for future progress is unlimited, as people master the art of true thinking.

There are still many skeptics who doubt that thought is creative. Consider, however, that in remote times there would have been many skeptics who reasoned as follows: "You can't stick seeds into the ground and expect something to grow from them. That is not how the world works! If you want to eat plants, you have to go out and gather them."

Sometimes, however, people stumble upon the positive use of a law. As with any natural law, it is self-enforcing, and works whether we define it consciously or not. For example, it is not necessary to conceptualize the law of gravity in order to throw a ball into the air, and have it return to Earth. It is not necessary to conceptualize the law of creative consciousness for a sales manager to prosper, if he genuinely believes in his products and confidently expects sales to increase. Similarly, the ailing woman, though not schooled in creative consciousness, applied the law in a positive way and was healed.

In all likelihood, the woman's greatest need was to advance beyond her own religious training. She had to put aside concepts and traditions that tended to block healing. "The woman, knowing what had been done to her, came in fear and trembling and fell down before him, and told him the whole truth." (Mark 5:33) While the expression "fear and trembling" was often used as poetic metaphor, as in Paul's letters, this would not apply here. We can easily account for actual fear and trembling when we view the situation *from her point of view*. She had just broken the Levitical Law by touching Jesus and many other people near him. In her desperation, she had deliberately crossed the line between "cleanness" and "uncleanness." Though she had been healed and knew it, there was the possibility–according to her own belief system–that she had received a healing contrary to the will of God.

Jesus made no reference here to the Book of Leviticus. Instead, he declared her to be permanently healed through her own exercise of faith. He understood that God's healing action is omnipresent, never limited to a given religion, set of doctrines, or system of ritual.

Original Christianity, at its core, was a ministry of healing and deliverance, and it still is where validly practiced. Nevertheless, over the centuries doctrines have developed that tend not to wholeness, but to mental and physical illness and decline. Those who teach depravity and separation from God tend to make people sick and sinful, not to heal them or to deliver them from their sins. In fact, countless people have gone like sheep to the slaughter, facing disability and premature death rather than correcting their views on how the spiritual universe works. Such crystallized forms of belief tend to be dignified by self-righteous attitudes and a false sense of loyalty. This is exactly where their mischief lies.

The situation today is mixed, but hopeful. Our current era is suffering from moral, spiritual, and intellectual decadence. "My people are destroyed for lack of knowledge." (Hosea 4:6) Yet it is also an era in which people are awakening to a consciousness of God's Presence and Power in the midst of them. Millions are experiencing spiritual healing and renewal, as God's healing grace is seen to be available to all. Ephesians 5:14 presents the challenge: "Awake, O sleeper, and arise from the dead, and Christ shall give you light." It is joyful to realize that many *are* awakening into the light.

Yes, the Divine Word or Healing Christ is here and available, in Its eternal and unconditioned state, ever active, ever prepared to breathe Its life, strength, and peace into us, even to incarnate Itself through us. It is the Open Door that no one can shut. Friends, this is not the Dark Ages, it is the 21st Century. Receive, then, the universal nature of Jesus' healing truth into your consciousness, and reject the folly of slamming the door shut on yourself.

Chapter 10

Raising of Jairus's Daughter

21When Jesus had crossed again in the boat to the other side, a great crowd gathered about him; and he was beside the sea. 22Then came one of the rulers of the synagogue, Jairus by name; and seeing him, he fell at his feet, 23and besought him, saying, "My little daughter is at the point of death. Come and lay your hands on her, so that she may be made well, and live." 24And he went with him. And a great crowd followed him and pressed round him....35While he was yet speaking, there came from the ruler's house some who said, "Your daughter is dead. Why trouble the Teacher any further?" 36But ignoring what they said, Jesus said to the ruler of the synagogue, "Do not fear; only believe." 37And he allowed no one to follow him except Peter and James and John the brother of James. 38When they came to the house of the ruler of the synagogue, he saw a tumult, and people weeping and wailing loudly. 39And when he had entered, he said to them, "Why do you make a tumult and weep? The child is not dead but sleeping." 40And they laughed at him. But he put them all outside, and took the child's father and mother and those who were with him, and went in where the child was. 41Taking her by the hand, he said to her, "Talitha cumi"; which means, "Little girl, I say to you, arise." 42And immediately the girl got up and walked; for she was twelve years old." And immediately they were overcome with amazement. 43And he strictly charged them that no one should know this, and told them to give her something to eat.
–Mark 5:21-24, 35-43 (parallel passages: Matthew 9:18-19, 23-26; Luke 8:40-42, 49-56)

This account can be taken either as a healing or as a resurrection. Yet Jesus plainly contrasted sleeping and death in this instance, saying, "The child is not dead but sleeping." (5:39) This is different from the resurrection at Nain, where a man's having died is not disputed. (Luke 7:11-17) Apparently the girl was in a kind of coma, with her etheric and physical bodies still connected. Jesus would have sensed this clairvoyantly. Also, after the girl revived, he "told them to give her something to eat." (5:43) Some theologians have interpreted this as a reference to the Lord's Supper. This, however, seems contrived, and is unacceptable from a historian's point of view. In addition, when children have successfully passed through a disease crisis, they are hungry and ask for food. The account shows Jesus caring for a child in a very human way.

Medical patients have been in comas for months and even years. We are not belittling the event by calling it a healing instead of a resurrection.

People who sincerely desire to understand Jesus better, especially his ways of working with the public, will find real answers here. With this end in mind, let us divide the record into its component parts.

While he was still speaking, there came from the ruler's house some who said, "Your daughter is dead. Why trouble the Teacher any further?" But ignoring what they said, Jesus said to the ruler of the synagogue, "Do not fear, only believe." (Mark 5:35-36)

The verb translated "ignoring" (*parakouo*) has a variety of meanings. It can mean to hear in a careless way, to pretend not to hear, or to disobey. If we are heeding the Christ within, we will ignore and disobey any negative comments that would deny the power and direction of our healing affirmations. We think and say "no" to any negative statements. What is more, we think and say "no" to our own doubts, fears, and negative images. We place ourselves above any distracting chatter, whether within or without, and focus on the Omnipresence of God.

Also, Jesus' statement, "Do not fear; only believe," is more accurately translated, "Stop being afraid, and continue to trust." This statement is in the present imperative tense, which implies continuous action. In modern terms, he told Jairus to mentally "shift gears" from doubt and fear to faith and trust. He was not told to *fight* his doubts and fears. If he shifted his thoughts in a positive direction, his emotions would follow. He was to look beyond the appearance of death to the reality of the Divine Presence and Life, especially in the child.

Affirm:

I SAY NO TO DOUBT AND FEAR. THE LIVING GOD FUNCTIONS THROUGH ME AS FAITH , CONFIDENCE, AND TRUST.

I AM FREE FROM THE PAST, AND FROM THE MISTAKES OF THE PAST. I ACCEPT THE HEALING PRESENCE AND POWER OF GOD WITHIN ME.

THE LIFE OF GOD HEALS AND RENEWS ME IN MIND AND BODY. I AM WHOLE, STRONG, AND WELL.

Continue to practice the thoughts and attitudes expressed here. It is not enough to just use a few affirmations, and to let one's thoughts run rampant afterwards. Continuing to trust in God in a practical sense is vitally important, and it takes continuous practice. Only in this way do we unfold an established consciousness of health.

And he allowed no one to follow him except Peter and James and John the brother of James. (Mark 5:37)

These three men were the hard core of Jesus' inner circle. He would have worked privately to help his closest disciples unfold a healing consciousness. It is apparent that he had a way of attuning the consciousness of Peter, James, and John to his own realization of God's Presence. As a result of this attunement, far greater results were generated. In the same way, people in healing work today are more effective when they have others who are closely attuned with them and with the Divine Presence.

When people unite in thought, feeling and imagery toward a given goal, tremendous results ensue. It is possible to collectively curse as well as bless, but the negative results of cursing rebound on those who do it with dire consequences. "What goes around comes around," and people reap what they sow, whether that be positive *or* negative. We are reminded of the words attributed to Moses: "I call heaven and earth to witness against you this day, that I have set before you life and death, blessing and curse; therefore choose life, that you and your descendants may live." (Deuteronomy 30:19)

The law involved is specific, and it exceeds even the potentials of $e=mc^2$. This formula quantifies the effects of collective thought, feeling, and imagery, which can be utilized for any positive purpose. *Other things being equal, the amount of transformative energy generated equals the number of individuals involved, plus the connections among all the individuals (each given the value of one).*

The formula is as follows:

x = the number of people involved

y = the amount of energy being generated

(x squared minus x) is divided by two. Then x is added. This equals y.

$$\frac{x^2 - x}{2} + x = y$$

This formula works in every case. It can be illustrated as follows:

If one person is involved, x=1. One squared is still one. 1 minus 1 = zero. Zero divided by 2 is still zero. Add 1 and we are back to 1 person.

If two persons are involved, x=2. 2 squared=4. 4 minus 2=2. 2 divided by 2=1. Add 2 to 1, and the result is 3. We have two individuals involved, and the connection between them counts as one, which also adds to 3.

If three persons are involved, x=3. 3 squared=9. 9 minus 3=6. 6 divided by 2=3. Add 3 to 3, and the result is 6. We have three individuals involved, and the connections among them count as three, which also adds to 6.

If four persons are involved, (as when Jesus, James, Peter, and John worked in unison), x=4. 4 squared=16. 16-4=12. 12 divided by 2=6. Add 6 to 4, and the result is 10. We have four individuals involved, and the connections among them count as six, which also adds to 10.

If 100 persons are involved, the multiplier effect of this law becomes more apparent. If x=100, x squared=10,000. 10,000 minus 100 is 9,900. 9,900 divided by 2=4,950. Add 100, the number of individuals involved, and the result is 5,050.

If 1000 persons are involved, the increase is even more dramatic. If x=1000, x squared =1,000,000. 1,000,000 minus 1000=999,000. 999,000 divided by 2=499,500. Add 1000, the number of individuals involved, to 499,500, and the result is 500,500.

If 10,000 persons are involved, the increase becomes extraordinary. If x=10,000, 10,000 squared=100,000,000. 100,000,000 minus 10,000=99,990,000. 99,990,00 divided by 2=49,995,000. Add 10,000, the number of individuals involved, and the result is 50,005,000.

Buckminster Fuller came close to discovering this law, but he did not factor in the number of individuals involved as the final step of the calculation. Of course, the more people who are involved in a given calculation, the less will be the *percentage* of distortion in not calculating the final step.

In the Unity tradition of interpretation, Peter is a symbol of faith, James is a symbol of wisdom, and John is a symbol of love, especially of Divine Love active within us. These are key ideas in the Mind of God. They are central to our own spiritual being. It is of great value to affirm, *individually and collectively,* that these qualities are alive and active within our own consciousness.

Let us affirm:

I HAVE THE FAITH OF JESUS CHRIST. I AM FAITH IN ACTION.

I HAVE THE WISDOM OF JESUS CHRIST. I AM WISDOM IN ACTION.

I HAVE THE LOVE OF JESUS CHRIST. I AM LOVE IN ACTION.

Let us consider, above all else, that when the Love of the Healing Christ is active in our souls, many healings will and do occur.

When they came to the house of the ruler of the synagogue, he saw a tumult, and people weeping and wailing loudly. And when he had entered, he said to them, "Why do you make a tumult and weep? The child is not dead but sleeping." And they laughed at him. But he put them all outside, and took the child's father and mother and those who were with them, and went in where the child was. (Mark 5:38-40)

The word translated "saw" (*theoreo*) means not only to see, but *to look at with interest and to examine carefully.* An experienced practitioner takes the time to survey a situation, and then follows up with appropriate action. It is basic to consider who and what to include in a healing situation, and also who and what to leave out. This includes the people, the outer setting and the contents of one's own consciousness. Every situation is unique and has its own requirements.

Jesus asked the people in Jairus's house, "Why do you make a tumult and weep?" This was a rhetorical question, for he already knew the answer. They did so because they were paid to do it. Both the Romans and the Jews hired mourners for funerals, who lamented as loudly and as sorrowfully as they could—a way to make a few drachmas. Jesus' first step was obvious, which was to insist that the mourners leave the house. Jairus, the owner, was pleased to cooperate in evicting them. It is important that you, too, cooperate with a qualified practitioner's wishes, when he or she comes to your house to guide you or another family member toward healing.

To do your own inner work in prayer and meditation, select a place that is quiet and orderly. Arrange the situation to remove any obstacles and distractions. Turn off television sets, radios, and other distracting devices. As Jesus taught, "When you pray, go into your room and shut the door and pray to your Father who is in secret; and your Father who sees in secret will reward you." (Matthew 6:6)

This statement, however, refers even more to inner preparation than to the outer environment of sight and sound. You will need to evict any thoughts or images that contradict the Divine reality which you are seeking to realize. Especially cast out doubts, such as "It can't be done." Remind yourself that you are not depending on your own personal merit or skills, but on the unlimited wisdom and power of God.

In Mark 5:40, the word translated "took" (*paralambano*) gives a vital clue to Jesus' success on this occasion. Its meaning is "to take under one's care and direction." Jesus took the girl's parents—as well as Peter, James, and John—under his spiritual care and direction. The parents, especially, needed guidance and stability at what was a critical moment for them, and they responded with confidence and trust.

*Taking her by the hand, he said to her, "Talitha cumi";
which means, "Little girl, I say to you, arise." And immediately*

the girl got up and walked; for she was twelve years old. And immediately they were overcome with amazement." (Mark 5:41-42)

An essential need in permanent healing is to change the contents of the subconscious phase of mind, to dissolve discord and to establish God's harmonious ideas. As already noted, the girl had been in a coma. When the conscious phase of mind is asleep, resistance to healing is diminished and marvelous results often occur. The subconscious never sleeps. The child awoke in response to Jesus' positive words.

One way to help a family member or friend is to arrange to be with the person when he or she is asleep. Then you can use affirmations to the greatest healing advantage. Speak softly, but firmly. Affirm his or her identity with the Word, the Indwelling Christ, and oneness with Divine Life unfolding from and within the Christ. You can also ask another to do this for you. Another method is to record affirmations on tape, and then play them when you are asleep.

The symbology of Verses 41 and 42 is quite remarkable. As in the case of Jesus' mother-in-law, the patient lies prone, is touched by Jesus, and then raised up. Here, too, we have an image of awakening from a limiting and discordant belief system into the light of true understanding.

The name of *Jairus*, the owner of the house, means "whom he (God) enlightens; vision; enlightenment." Our true home, in a spiritual sense, is a vision of oneness, wholeness, and harmony. This inner illumination completes us as an effective channel of healing.

The numbers 7 and 12 are also part of the symbology. Both numbers represent completion and fulfillment, as with the 7 days of creation and the 12 tribes of Israel. Seven people were in the house when the healing occurred: Jesus, Peter, James, John, Jairus, Jairus's wife, and the child herself. Also, the child is said to be 12 years old, and the woman in Mark 5:25 is said to have suffered for 12 years. Both were healed.

Jesus entering the house, and evicting the mourners, is the greatest symbol in the text. In a similar way, the Healing Christ enters our own souls. This means more than a specific healing; it is a healing consciousness which includes Peter (faith), James (wisdom), and John (love). To repeat, healings will occur when Divine Love, flowing through us and radiating from us, is strongly experienced. As Colossians 3:14 declares: "Above all these put on love, which binds everything together in perfect harmony."

"And he strictly charged them that no one should know this, and told them to give her something to eat." (Mark 5:43)

Telling them to give the child food was not only thoughtful, it was common sense, for she had recovered and her appetite had returned. It would be strange if she had not been hungry. What many readers question is why, in this situation, Jesus gave strict orders not to let people know about the healing. He had made quite a scene in clearing out the crowd, and there was no possible way of keeping this healing secret. There would have been a motley collection of disciples, curiosity seekers, scoffers, and mourners (some sincere, others hired) standing outside, waiting to find out what would happen.

The fact that Jesus spoke Aramaic on this occasion leads us to the answer. In Aramaic, with a certain inflection of the voice and appropriate gestures, the phrase "tell no one" means its exact opposite–*tell everyone*! Jesus, in advising them to keep the matter "hushed up," clearly intended the exact opposite meaning.

Chapter 11

Two Blind Men Indoors

27And as Jesus passed on from there, two blind men followed him, crying aloud, "Have mercy on us, Son of David." 28When he entered the house, the blind men came to him; and Jesus said to them, "Do you believe that I am able to do this?" They said to him, "Yes, Lord." 29Then he touched their eyes, saying, "According to your faith, be it done to you." 30And their eyes were opened. And Jesus sternly charged them, "See that no one knows it." 31But they went away and spread his fame through all that district.
–Matthew 9:27-31

How can God restore sight to the blind? Let us consider what it means to be All-in-all, using a modern illustration not available to Jesus or the Biblical writers. If a holographic plate is cut in pieces, each piece still contains the entire picture of the original. God is like a hologram, in which the whole picture is present in all the parts. That is to say, the "whole picture" of God's Allness is within every one of us and is the very nature of our being as Spirit, soul, and body. This wholeness includes perfect eyes and perfect everything. Being All-in-all can mean no less.

Even while maintaining this awesome vision, we need also to look at the Biblical records in a historical perspective. The above account appears only in the Gospel of Matthew, and its author wrote this gospel primarily for a Jewish audience. While noting that Jesus' message is for people of all nations (Matthew 28:19), the author nevertheless utilized Jewish literary practices.

One of the ways he did this was to double various events. This practice is reflected in the Old Testament in a variety of ways. For example, Psalms 62:11 declares:

"Once God has spoken;
twice have I heard this:
that power belongs to God."
Also, Job 42:10 reads:

"The Lord restored the fortunes of Job, when he had prayed for his friends; and the Lord gave Job twice as much as he had before."

The author of Matthew followed this pattern as he modified the material in the Gospel of Mark, which he used as a source document:

Mark 5:1-20 - one man; *Matthew 8:28-34* - two demoniacs
Mark 10:46-52 - Bartimaeus; *Matthew 20:29-34* - two blind men

Also, sharing an oral or written source with the Gospel of Luke:

Luke 11:14-23 - a dumb man speaks; *Matthew 9:32-34* and *12:22-24* - records the same event twice
Matthew 12:22-24 - makes him not only dumb, but also blind

Therefore, we can be reasonably certain that Jesus worked with only one man in the episode recorded in Matthew 9:27-31, to restore his sight. Of course, it is no less remarkable to restore the sight of one blind person at a given time, than to restore the sight of two.

All of the records of Jesus' healing work are valuable, even if modified, for they reveal something of the pattern of his activities. Here, Jesus made a point of contact with the one seeking help. It seems, however, that in this case, he needed little persuasion. He followed Jesus into the house, where the Master asked him, "Do you believe that I am able to do this?"[1] He answered, "Yes, Lord." He shared Jesus' *expectancy* that the healing would occur. Also, while Jesus did not deny his own part as a channel of healing, his way of questioning the man deepened the patient's own involvement in the healing process.

Expectancy is a key issue in recovery, no matter what method is used. This also applies to life in a larger sense. Therefore, *expect* your needs to be met as you are guided and illumined by the Indwelling Christ. Affirm:

GOD'S PRESENCE IS UNIVERSAL AND ETERNAL. THEREFORE, AS GOD'S CONSCIOUSNESS WORKS THROUGH ME:

I EXPECT TO BE HEALED.

I EXPECT TO BE GUIDED TO MY HIGHEST GOOD.

I EXPECT TO BE CAPABLE AND PROSPEROUS.

I EXPECT TO LOVE OTHERS, AND TO BE LOVED.

I EXPECT TO OVERCOME ERRORS AND FAULTS, AND TO DEVELOP POSITIVE HABITS IN THEIR PLACE.

I EXPECT GOD'S WONDERFUL PLAN TO UNFOLD IN MY LIFE.

I YIELD TO THE CHRIST WITHIN ME, IN PERFECT TRUST.

"He touched their [or his] eyes." (9:29) The laying on of hands, as we have seen, is a good idea where useful and appropriate. Jesus released definite energy in doing so, and also did something tangible with which the patient could relate. He was blind and could not see Jesus initially. He could, however, feel Jesus' fingers and sense the energy flowing through them. Nevertheless, his own expectancy and trust were vitally important. Note the shift in emphasis: "According to *your* faith [assurance, confidence, trust] be it done to you." (9:29)

"And their [or his] eyes were opened." (9:30) This refers not only to an external event, but also to opening spiritual vision. When his sight was restored, he saw Jesus. In a similar way, our personal selves, once blinded by ignorance and spiritual darkness, are made whole, conscious of their connection with the Indwelling Christ.

Affirm:

I HAVE DIRECT KNOWLEDGE OF TRUTH.

I HAVE SPIRITUAL INTUITION.

I LET THE TRANSFORMING POWER OF GOD'S LOVE CHANGE DARKNESS INTO LIGHT, AND I KNOW THE WAY.

Meditate on the following Bible passages:

"I AM THE LIGHT OF THE WORLD; HE WHO FOLLOWS ME WILL NOT WALK IN DARKNESS, BUT WILL HAVE THE LIGHT OF LIFE." (John 8:12)

"YOU ARE THE LIGHT OF THE WORLD. A CITY SET ON A HILL CANNOT BE HID." (Matthew 5:14)

"THIS IS THE MESSAGE WE HAVE HEARD FROM HIM, AND PROCLAIM TO YOU, THAT GOD IS LIGHT AND IN HIM IS NO DARKNESS AT ALL." (I John 1:5)

"Jesus sternly charged them [or him], 'See that no one knows it.'" (9:30) In this instance, the blind man had his sight restored in private. This is in sharp contrast with many other healings, which occurred in the presence of large numbers of people. When Jesus told him, "See that no one knows it," he was not joking as in the case of Jairus's daughter. He really meant that he was not to discuss his restored sight with others. The fact that he ignored Jesus' instruction does not negate the purpose behind it, which was for the man's own good.

As far as is known, no child, having awakened from a coma, has ever been coaxed back into the same type of unconsciousness by foolish people. Adults healed of chronic conditions have, however, sometimes been led back into their former condition by scoffers and unbelievers.

The real question is: *After you have had a healing, then what?* Some people will rejoice with you. On the other hand, some family members, friends, or business associates may not be interested in, or favorable to, spiritual healing. This applies especially when a chronic disease, disability, or addiction has been overcome. You are not the only one who changes if your sight returns, your ability to walk is restored, a life-threatening condition is healed, or you recover from an addiction. Others have been used to having you in a certain way. Now that you have changed, they too will have to change their perceptions of you, and also of themselves and their own social or care-giving roles.

It is best, then, not to discuss your healing with the general public, or even with certain people who are close to you. Call it

91

a miracle if you want to, or say "I thank God for it," but do not elaborate. Instead, quietly carry out a positive pattern of thought, imagery, word, and action, and do it every day and every hour of the day.

Strictly avoid focusing on past symptoms. Also, never under any circumstances make preparations for a possible relapse. Such a negative focus or preparation has a good chance of recreating the condition from which you have now become freed. If you have fled without injury from a burning building, you would be foolish indeed to run back into it. Similarly, it is simply idiotic to reinstate a negative pattern in one's own consciousness.

Another question that may arise is: Shall I make a public testimonial about my healing at a meeting or service scheduled to give people this opportunity? Yes, by all means do so, for on such occasions, people have come together for this specific purpose.

Rhea White, a prominent member of the Academy of Religion and Psychical Research, points out that testifying to "exceptional human experiences" (and healing of blindness by spiritual means would certainly qualify) has a positive value both for the individual and for the larger society. It helps the speaker, as well as those addressed, to become more firmly grounded in a new mind-set of wholeness and spiritual well-being. Thus, testimonial meetings are an obvious exception to the caution required in discussing a given healing. Rhea White notes:

"We can take the easy route of unquestioningly accepting society's norm by doubting, questioning, minimizing, ignoring, suppressing, and even repressing, that is, forgetting, our exceptional human experiences, thereby reinforcing the role of the doubters in our society; or we can honor our experiences, revel in them, love them, share them,

92

and in any way we can, believe in and foster them, thereby reinforcing the role of the believers and affirmers. Whichever role we choose to play will have an impact on society at large. We will add our influence to it, one way or another."**2**

It would, of course, be a mistake to try to use a testimonial meeting merely to draw attention to oneself, though few actually do this. The goal is to praise the healing Presence of God, not to take any personal credit or portray ourselves as "holier than thou." We praise the One; we do not practice one-upmanship.

Testimonials end, but the need remains, day by day, to live out the true meaning of our lives–to think and live with spiritual vision. There is no better post-recovery advice than that of Paul in Philippians 3:13-14: "Forgetting what lies behind and straining forward to what lies ahead, I press on toward the goal for the prize of the upward call of God in Christ Jesus."

Chapter 12

The Syrophoenician Woman's Daughter

24From there he arose and went away to the region of Tyre and Sidon. And he entered a house, and would not have any one know it; yet he could not be hid. 25But immediately a woman, whose little daughter was possessed by an unclean spirit, heard of him, and came and fell down at his feet. 26Now the woman was a Greek, a Syrophoenician by birth. And she begged him to cast the demon out of her daughter. 27And he said to her, "Let the children first be fed, for it is not right to take the children's bread and throw it to the dogs." 28But she answered him, "Yes, Lord; yet even the dogs under the table eat the children's crumbs." 29And he said to her, "For this saying you may go your way; the demon has left your daughter." 30And she went home, and found the child lying in bed, and the demon gone.
–Mark 7:24-30 (parallel passage: Matthew 15:21-28)

The Gospel of Luke does not record this event, so it was probably not in the urtext of Mark that Luke used as a source. In its written form, then, the text is probably further removed in time from the actual occurrence. Even so, its joyful nature is apparent, despite less positive interpretations that are sometimes offered.

Jesus understood the importance of going apart by himself at times, to rest, meditate, and become spiritually renewed through communion with God. He then returned to his ministry with renewed insight and power. Also, on at least one occasion, he took a vacation in another country, Phoenicia. He sought a relaxed atmosphere where he could relate to people not as a

95

teacher and healer, but simply as a fellow human being. The account in the Gospel of Matthew mentions unnamed "disciples," but none are mentioned in Mark's version, which is earlier and more accurate. Yes, Jesus wanted a vacation, but his fame had preceded him and he was not fully successful. Mark 3:8 tells us that some members of the crowds that followed him were from Tyre and Sidon, the two main Phoenician cities on the Mediterranean coast.

The woman who sought his help was a Greek by language and culture. She was a Phoenician of the original Syrian homeland, rather than of North Africa–hence the term Syrophoenician. A close look at the text also shows that Jesus spoke Greek on this occasion.

Mark's record indicates a relaxed and joyful mood. It reflects the inner joy that was basic to Jesus' character. In fact, we find a distinct casualness and spontaneity in the way he trusted God for healing. He sensed inwardly that it was done, and it was done.

To this day, some of the easiest yet greatest healings–whether for self or for others–come to pass in a relaxed and spontaneous state of consciousness, inspired by the Indwelling God. Manuals, textbooks, and other written guides can be a real help. Yet there are times to put the books aside and to simply move inwardly with God's healing action.

The Gospel of Mark tells us that "He entered a house and would not have any one know it, yet he could not be hid." (7:24) Evidently, some of the more well-to-do Phoenicians had guest rooms for rent. Jesus was tired and needed peace and quiet after a period of intensive activity. By vacationing in a non-Jewish house, he discouraged his followers from intruding.

The account is unusual in its use of diminutive terms, including the Greek words for *little* dogs, *little* children, and *little* morsels. This shows that the conversation between Jesus and the woman was light-hearted and casual. Evidently, Jesus ate dinner with the local family where he stayed, which included some children and their canine pets. The Syrophoenician woman, hearing that the great healer was in town, came to him while he was eating and begged him to heal her daughter. Evidently, these youngsters slipped some food to their little pets from time to time. There is no sense of separation here, but a delight in sharing. The point of the text is that the spiritual insights of Jesus and the prophets (the children) are to be freely and joyfully shared with all humanity (the puppies).

"And she went home, and found the child lying in bed, and the demon gone." (7:30) In this context, lying down does not represent spiritual ignorance. It has the sense of rest, relaxation, and release from tension. The Greek word for lying down is *kline*, which is from *klino*, meaning "to rest; to cause to yield." To heal is to release, to allow to be adjusted. As Jesus spoke the word with spontaneous trust in the Divine Presence, and the girl's mother gave up her anxious concern, the healing was done.

There is a common pattern in four accounts: The official's son (John 4:46-54), Jairus's daughter (Mark 5:21-24, 35-43), the epileptic boy (Mark 9:14-29, to be discussed in Chapter 15), and the present case in Mark 7:24-30. In each we find an anxious parent asking Jesus for help. Parental anxiety is often the hidden factor behind a child's illness and its continuation. We must be totally frank about this. Fear and anxiety sometimes hurt and, in extreme cases, can even kill the very person one most earnestly desires to help or protect. This applies whether or not the people involved are physically in the same place–and most strongly, as in this instance, between a mother and child. The tie is basically emotional. Therefore, if you have a sick child, spouse, relative, or close friend, consider whether you have a basic need to release your concern, to let go and let God.

There is, of course, a positive side to this. Parents, when they affirm and mentally picture a child healthy and strong, become a potent factor for healing. This is also apparent in the Gospels, as well as in contemporary healing practice.

We will be just as frank on the positive side. We know *that* Jesus loved children, but we might also consider *how* Jesus loved children. For example, if we can love a little girl or boy on a human level as one who goes to school in the morning, returns home in the afternoon, enjoys a hot meal, and then rests by a warm fire, that is good. If we can love this same child as a free spirit, in essence infinite and eternal, that is also good. If we can love the child in both ways at the same time, we are truly seeing as God sees, and loving as God loves. Let us remember that health in all things is God's energy made visible. Jesus was aware of this, which also gave him clearer insight into the law of creative consciousness, and how it works in every aspect of our everyday lives.

When we say, "Your child is God's child," it is not a cliche. We really mean it. Affirm for the person who needs healing, especially if you are one of the parents:

_____ IS GOD'S CHILD. (S)HE IS CREATED, SUSTAINED, AND MAINTAINED BY THE ENERGY AND VITALITY OF SPIRIT. THROUGH THE SPIRIT OF GOD IN HIM(HER), (S)HE IS NOW RESPONDING TO GOD'S HEALING LOVE.

While it is not a good idea to become flippant about health concerns, sometimes healing work does call for a lighter touch. This is what we find in this account. Jesus released healing by making light of the problem and bringing joy to the situation. Norman Cousins, who proved in his own life how joy and humor can contribute to recovery, quoted an old proverb of unknown origin: "A good clown will do more for a town's health than 20 asses laden with drugs."

Proverbs 17:22 declares:

"A cheerful heart is a good medicine,
But a downcast spirit dries up the bones."

The joy of Spirit, which wells up within us, is meant to be a mainspring of our consciousness of well-being. As Paul observed, "The fruit of the Spirit is love, joy, peace, patience, kindness, goodness, faithfulness, gentleness, self-control." (Galatians 5:22-23)

In the story of Pollyanna, the little girl reminds her minister about the "glad passages" in the Bible. This is not sentiment, but fact. The Bible calls on us to experience joy as a gift of God.

Meditate on the following:

"DO NOT BE GRIEVED, FOR THE JOY OF THE LORD IS YOUR STRENGTH." (Nehemiah 8:10)

"THOU DOST SHOW ME THE PATH OF LIFE; IN THY PRESENCE THERE IS FULNESS OF JOY, IN THY RIGHT HAND ARE PLEASURES FOR EVERMORE." (Psalms 16:11)

"WEEPING MAY TARRY FOR THE NIGHT, BUT JOY COMES WITH THE MORNING." (Psalms 30:5)

"WITH JOY YOU WILL DRAW WATERS FROM THE WELLS OF SALVATION." (Isaiah 12:3)

"AND THE RANSOMED OF THE LORD SHALL RETURN, AND COME TO ZION WITH SINGING; EVERLASTING JOY SHALL BE UPON THEIR HEADS; THEY SHALL OBTAIN JOY AND GLADNESS, AND SORROW AND SIGHING SHALL FLEE AWAY."–Isaiah 35:10; 51:11

"THESE THINGS I HAVE SPOKEN TO YOU, THAT MY JOY MAY BE IN YOU, AND THAT YOUR JOY MAY BE FULL." (John 15:11)

"YOUR HEARTS WILL REJOICE, AND NO ONE WILL TAKE YOUR JOY FROM YOU." (John 16:22)

"HITHERTO YOU HAVE ASKED NOTHING IN MY NAME; ASK, AND YOU WILL RECEIVE, THAT YOUR JOY MAY BE FULL." (John 16:24)

"THE KINGDOM OF GOD DOES NOT MEAN FOOD AND DRINK BUT RIGHTEOUSNESS AND PEACE AND JOY IN THE HOLY SPIRIT." (Romans 14:17)

"REJOICE IN THE LORD ALWAYS; AGAIN I WILL SAY, REJOICE." (Philippians 4:4)

Chapter 13

Deaf Man with Speech Impediment

31Then he returned from the region of Tyre, and went through Sidon to the Sea of Galilee, through the region of the Decapolis. 32And they brought to him a man who was deaf and had an impediment in his speech; and they besought him to lay his hand upon him. 33And, taking him aside from the multitude privately, he put his fingers into his ears, and he spat and touched his tongue; 34and looking up to heaven, he sighed, and said to him, "Ephphatha," that is, "Be opened." 35And his ears were opened, his tongue was released, and he spoke plainly. 36And he charged them to tell no one; but the more he charged them, the more zealously they proclaimed it. 37And they were astonished beyond measure saying, "He has done all things well; he even makes the deaf hear and the dumb speak."
–Mark 7:31-37

We cannot know the route that Jesus took in traveling from Sidon to the Sea of Galilee. If the sequence in the Gospel of Mark between Phoenicia and the Decapolis is historically accurate, it is quite possible that Jesus spent some time in the mountains of Syria. This would have finally given him a chance to meditate and commune with God without any interruptions.

Decapolis is a Greek word meaning "ten cities." Located southeast of the Sea of Galilee, the area contained a league of ten cities of Greek culture. Although the Decapolis was part of the Roman Empire, each city governed its own local affairs.

101

According to this account, Jesus acted in ways contrary to his usual methods. The form of his actions resembles that of Greek magicians, who sought for an alien power to come into a patient and heal him. In this instance, he took a series of seven actions:

(1) He led the patient aside privately. This kept him from being embarrassed by onlookers. It enabled Jesus to work with him to remove fear and tension.
(2) He put his fingers into the man's ears.
(3) He used saliva. According to ancient traditions, the patient would have expected this to have a magical effect.
(4) He touched the man's tongue.
(5) He looked upward.
(6) He sighed.
(7) He declared, "Be opened."

Even in this series of actions, however, Jesus affirmed the spiritual basis of healing, rather than the magical concept of bringing a force in from the outside. Note that he first looked up at the sky and then declared, "Be opened." The Aramaic term *ephphatha*, translated "be opened," implies openness to heaven, meaning the omnipresent realm of Divine ideas from which all healing comes forth. *Ephphatha* is related to the Hebrew verb, *pathach*, which means "to open wide." It has the sense of "to loosen, appear, break forth, draw out, let go free." That is to say, the Divine state of perfection is already present, and the work of a Christian healer is to release this present reality into expression through his or her own trust and inner attunement.

Considering the unique situation, we can see that Jesus had two reasons for taking unusual steps. First, the man lived in a Hellenistic area where people expected healers to act much as he did on this occasion. Second, the man was deaf, so *Jesus had to communicate with him in nonverbal ways*. His actions, then, were an instrument of the moment, used to establish rapport with the man needing help.

Again and again, in these healing records, Jesus deals with the central issue of how the individual views himself or herself. This is not unlike modern counseling concepts. The difference, and the secret of Jesus' greater effectiveness, is the decisive way that he turned mentally from the outer appearance of sin, sickness, and disability, and focused on the essential oneness of the patient with God. Instead of fighting the condition, he let God's perfect idea, the Christ, show forth in and through the patient.

We find that the patient had some ability to speak, but did so with difficulty. He suffered not only from deafness, but also most likely from stuttering. In the medical field today, there are two diametrically opposed schools of thought about the cause and cure of stuttering. Basically, the dispute is whether to use physical or psychological methods in working with such patients toward a cure. This book is not intended to intervene in medical disputes, and will not do so. It is, however, the purpose of this book to review how Jesus worked to release wholeness in people's lives.

It is apparent that Jesus approached this problem, and its solution, from a spiritual *and* psychological point of view. Even the saliva was used to bolster the patient's confidence, not as a true therapeutic agent. Jesus had to somehow communicate a new image of self to the man needing help. This was not an easy challenge, but apparently he succeeded in doing so. The patient moved beyond the self-image of being "a stutterer," and realized on some level that he had a divine inheritance as a child of God.

It was necessary to break up a negative cycle consisting of four steps:

(1) Low self-esteem led to (2) fear, which produced (3) tension, which in turn resulted in (4) stuttering, which reinforced (1) low self-esteem and continued the cycle.

People try to heal problems of this nature–or destructive habits of any kind–by will power, but this is a trap. *If people are not told that letting go and letting the grace of God function is basically the way out, they may never figure it out for themselves.* Their whole lives can thus be destroyed, as in the case of an alcoholic who loses everything: his health, his family, the respect of his friends and community, his home, and his career.

We need to remove Ephesians 2:8-9 out of a formal theological context, and consider its practical, therapeutic point: "By grace, you have been saved [healed, made whole] through faith [yielding, trust]; and it is not your own doing [by will power], it is the gift of God–not because of works [personal efforts], lest any man should boast."

Affirm:

"THERE IS, THEREFORE, NO CONDEMNATION FOR THOSE WHO ARE IN CHRIST JESUS." (Romans 8:1)

I TOTALLY REJECT THE FALSE SELF-IMAGE OF SIN. I AM ONE WITH GOD'S INTEGRITY. I AM ONE WITH GOD'S RIGHTEOUSNESS.

I TOTALLY REJECT THE FALSE SELF-IMAGE OF SICKNESS. I AM ONE WITH GOD'S WHOLENESS. I AM ONE WITH GOD'S STRENGTH.

I TOTALLY REJECT THE FALSE SELF-IMAGE OF IGNORANCE. I AM ONE WITH GOD'S WISDOM. I AM ONE WITH GOD'S KNOWLEDGE.

I TOTALLY REJECT THE FALSE SELF-IMAGE OF LACK. I AM ONE WITH GOD'S PRODUCTIVE NATURE. I AM ONE WITH GOD'S ABUNDANT SUPPLY.

I AM GOD'S PERFECT IDEA, FIRST, LAST, AND ALWAYS. I CLAIM THIS FREEING TRUTH FOR MYSELF. I KNOW THE TRUTH, AND THE TRUTH MAKES ME FREE. I AM NOW FREE WITH THE FREEDOM OF SPIRIT.

Mark 7:36 declares, "He [Jesus] charged them to tell no one." What are we to make of this call to secrecy? In the case of Jairus's daughter, he intended this as satire, meaning "tell everyone." In the healing of blindness in Matthew 9:27-31, he wanted it kept quiet for the patient's benefit, so that the patient would not unwittingly recreate the problem. In this instance, however, Jesus acted partly out of self-interest. The Greek of this passage is in the middle voice. In Greek, a command given in the middle voice meant that one is speaking in his own interests.

Jesus never compromised his principles, but neither did he see a need to go out of his way to invite trouble. His intended secrecy had to do partly with preserving the healing itself, and partly with the unusual methods he used in this given case. These quasi-magical gestures bordered on the illegal according to Roman laws. His chances of being taken to court for this type of activity were greater in the Decapolis. Galilee was a hotbed of rebellion, and most of its rural inhabitants had little use for Roman law. By contrast, citizens of the Decapolis strongly supported the Roman rule. They were like Americans in the former Panama Canal Zone, more ostensibly patriotic than people living in the fifty states.

Despite Jesus' call for secrecy, word of the healing spread quickly. "They were astonished beyond measure, saying, 'He has done all things well (*kalos*); he even makes the deaf hear and the dumb speak.'" (Mark 7:37) The deep structure of ancient Greek, just below its surface, carried the subliminal insight that the energy of life unfolds from the inside out, from center to circumference, from consciousness to action and condition. And when the text uses the adverb *kalos*, it tells us that Jesus did his works *as the outward sign or expression of an inward state of goodness, honor, and nobility.* Whether used as an adjective or in an adverbial context, it is what the word *kalos* means. This basic, freeing insight, as practiced by Jesus, is also the key to making our lives a fuller expression of our highest potential here and now, today.

Chapter 14

Blind Man at Bethsaida

22And they came to Bethsaida. And some people brought to him a blind man, and begged him to touch him. 23And he took the blind man by the hand, and led him out of the village; and when he had spit on his eyes and laid his hands upon him, he asked him, "Do you see anything?" 24And he looked up and said, "I see men; but they look like trees, walking." 25Then again he laid his hands upon his eyes; and he looked intently and was restored, and saw everything clearly. 26And he sent him away to his home saying, "Do not even enter the village."
–Mark 8:22-26

People involved in the healing ministry meet all types. It is rare, though not unheard of, for patients to take Divine healing *too* much for granted. Even if they recover from a life-threatening illness, they lack a decent appreciation for God's healing action. This can be exasperating. Jesus rarely lost his temper, but that he did so regarding the people of Bethsaida, and another town, may be based on a historical memory. Luke 10:13 has him declare: "Woe to you, Chorazin! Woe to you, Bethsaida! for if the mighty works done in you had been done in Tyre and Sidon, they would have repented long ago, sitting in sackcloth and ashes."

While we have written much about the Healing Christ as a universal reality, the personal Jesus continues to live in his resurrected state, and still may act when called upon for help. For example, there was a case in which a little boy had badly damaged an eye, which an ophthalmologist said was hopeless to save. After a minister specifically called on Jesus for help, however, his eye and his sight were quickly and totally restored. The boy's grandmother responded to the healing with great joy, but it became a source of dread to the ignorant, who regarded it as the work of an evil wizard rather than a dedicated Christian working with the greatest healer of all. This parallels the accusation against Jesus that "He casts out demons by Beelzebul, the prince of demons." (Luke 11:15)

In the case of the blind man in Mark 8:22-26, Jesus led him away from Bethsaida and worked with him in private. He spat on his eyes and laid his hands upon him. Many people believed that holy men and chiefs of state could cure blindness by using their saliva as a healing agent. While saliva cannot heal blindness, the power of belief and of expectation is so far-reaching that this sometimes occurred.

In English, we have the idiom, "licking his wounds," apparently a trace of this ancient form of belief. Animals actually lick their wounds in many cases, acting by instinct. Though saliva may accelerate the healing process, Jesus no doubt took this action to increase the man's expectancy that he would receive his sight. This made him more receptive to Jesus' realization of God's Presence and Power. Certainly the Divine Intelligence that designed the human eye knows how to fully restore it.

Affirm:

BY THE DIVINE LAW OF EXPRESSION, I SHOW FORTH PERFECT FORM AND FUNCTION IN MY BODY, AS A TOTAL UNITY IN HARMONY WITH SPIRIT.

GOD'S CLEANSING, HEALING, PURIFYING LOVE FLOWS FREELY THROUGH ME IN SOUL AND BODY,

RENEWING AND RESTORING ME.

THE RADIANT LIGHT OF CHRIST SHINES THROUGH EVERY CELL OF MY BODY. I AM WHOLE AND WELL.

Healings can be gradual; they do not need to be instantaneous. At first, the patient said, "I see men; but they look like trees, walking." (8:24) Only later did he see everything clearly. As noted in Chapter 8, the impression of being brief is made more acute when the Greek of the New Testament is translated into English. In this case, Jesus not only asked the man, "Do you see anything?" (8:23) *He did so earnestly and repeatedly.* His very effort and expectation to see, encouraged by Jesus, increased the likelihood of his seeing.

The effects of affirmative prayer and imaging often show themselves by degrees, rather than instantly. These effects can be cumulative. It is vitally important, however, that you continue in a positive state of mind and expectancy *during the times between prayers.* If you do so, the active energy will build up mightily and then, at a given point, emerge as a cure. If, instead, you let doubt and fear take over, you will cancel what has been accomplished and will have to start over from the beginning.

Let thoughts and images of love, good will, health, joy, and peace abide within you, not just at special times, but throughout the day. Note this statement from the Allegory of the Vine: "If you *abide* in me, and my words *abide* in you, ask whatever you will, and it shall be done for you." (John 15:7)

Declare:
I AM THE LIGHT OF THE WORLD. I GIVE THANKS THAT GOD IS NOW POURING IN TO MY CONSCIOUSNESS NEW LIGHT BY WHICH TO THINK, TO LIVE, AND TO GROW.

I AM A RADIATING CENTER OF LOVE, WISDOM, JOY, AND HEALING POWER.

FROM DEEP WITHIN, I NOW RADIATE THE PEACE, HARMONY, AND LOVE OF GOD.

THE PURE, UNLIMITED IDEAS OF DIVINE MIND ARE NOW RELEASED IN MY AWARENESS. I AM QUICKENED, RENEWED, AND ESTABLISHED IN A CONSCIOUSNESS OF WHOLENESS AND HARMONY.

Jesus understood, with complete clarity, that the springs of life are from within. The formative power of thought, feeling, and belief is always at work, shaping our outer conditions according to what we hold in mind. He also understood that the company we keep can either lift us up or drag us down in consciousness. Jesus, and people called to minister in His Name, and being well prepared to do so, tend to go wherever they are needed. In the case of the blind man, however, we are talking about something altogether different. It was necessary to get him to leave Bethsaida with its perverse attitudes and, having had his sight restored, to go directly home and not return to that village. At first, "he [Jesus] took the blind man by the hand, and led him out of the village." (8:23) Later, after receiving his sight, "he sent him away to his home, saying, "Do not even enter the village." (8:26)

People involved in healing work often divide human needs into three categories, and it is certainly proper to do so. These are *health*, *illumination*, and *prosperity*. Another is *harmonious relationships*, and this is sometimes added as a fourth category, given that a substantial number of prayer requests involve this area of need.

It became increasingly apparent after decades of practice, however, that *these four areas are interrelated and need to be viewed as such.* It is not enough if one is healed of a mental or physical condition, if he or she then returns to an unwholesome or hostile environment. Also, when people have to make major changes in their situation, they need not rely solely on their own personal judgment, or on that of other people. They can be *guided from within* to take the best course of action for all concerned, and then be *empowered from within* to do whatever is appropriate.

Affirm:

DIVINE ORDER AND RIGHT ACTION NOW GOVERN MY LIFE AND AFFAIRS.

I AM GUIDED IN ALL MY WAYS, AND I MAKE RIGHT DECISIONS.

I HAVE UNSHAKABLE FAITH IN THE PERFECT OUTCOME OF EVERY SITUATION IN MY LIFE, FOR I KNOW THAT GOD IS IN ABSOLUTE CONTROL.

GOD IS BRINGING ONLY GOOD TO PASS IN MY LIFE AND AFFAIRS, AND I AM PATIENT, POISED, AND OPTIMISTIC.

I NOW LET GO OF ALL THAT LIMITS ME, AND I LET GOD FILL MY LIFE WITH HIS GOOD.

Chapter 15

The Epileptic Boy

2After six days, Jesus took with him Peter and James and John, and led them up a high mountain apart by themselves; and he was transfigured before them, 3and his garments became glistening, intensely white, as no fuller on Earth could bleach them.
–Mark 9:2-3 (parallel passages: Matthew 17:1-2; Luke 9:28-29)

14And when they came to the disciples, they saw a great crowd about them, and scribes arguing with them. 15And immediately all the crowd, when they saw him, were greatly amazed, and ran up to him and greeted him. 16And he asked them, "What are you discussing with them?" 17And one of the crowd answered him, "Teacher, I brought my son to you, for he has a dumb spirit; 18and whenever it seizes him, it dashes him down; and he foams and grinds his teeth and becomes rigid; and I asked your disciples to cast it out, and they were not able." 19And he answered them, "O faithless generation, how long am I to be with you? How long am I to bear with you? Bring him to me." 20And they brought the boy to him; and when the spirit saw him, immediately it convulsed the boy, and he fell on the ground and rolled about, foaming at the mouth. 21And Jesus asked his father, "How long has he had this?" And he said, "From childhood. 22And it has often cast him into the fire and into the water, to destroy him; but if you can do anything, have pity on us and help us." 23And Jesus said to him, "If you can! All things are possible to him who believes." 24Immediately the father of the child cried out and said, "I believe; help my

113

unbelief!" 25And when Jesus saw that a crowd came running together, he rebuked the unclean spirit, saying to it, "You dumb and deaf spirit, I command you, come out of him, and never enter him again." 26And after crying out and convulsing him terribly, it came out, and the boy was like a corpse; so that most of them said, "He is dead." 27But Jesus took him by the hand and lifted him up, and he arose. 28And when he had entered the house, his disciples asked him privately, "Why could we not cast it out?" 29And he said to him, "This kind cannot be driven out by anything but prayer."
–Mark 9:14-29 (parallel passages: Matthew 17:14-21; Luke 9:37-43)

The Gospel of Mark paints a dramatic contrast between the transfiguration scene on the mountain, and the confused situation in the valley below. The mood shifts abruptly when Jesus, Peter, James, and John return to the valley. Divine order and harmony prevail on the mountain as light radiates from Jesus. Returning to the valley, they find chaos and confusion. The scribes are wrangling with the nine apostles who remained below. The nine had failed to heal an epileptic youth, and critics may also have taunted them that they were losing their power.

The mountain weaves its literal and symbolic aspects together. The cloud in Mark 9:7 represents the Shekinah, the Presence of God in Jewish tradition, as does the light. We can only speculate regarding the cloud's actual nature. To do so here would take us too far afield. The central event was the transfiguration of Jesus himself.

The verb translated "transfigured" (*metamorphoo*, related to the English word "metamorphosis") means *to give outer expression to one's inner nature and character*. It carries the basic image, "As within, so without." The mountain is a universal planetary symbol for a lofty state of spiritual consciousness. We also find that Jesus went up to the mountain "after six days," (9:2) that is to say, on the seventh day. Seven is a symbol of completion; God's work is completed and made manifest, as in Genesis 2:1-3. Moses and Elijah may have actually appeared; or their presence may be symbolic, a dramatic way of saying that Jesus has fulfilled the work of the law (represented by Moses) and the prophets (represented by Elijah). What we can be certain of is what the scene depicts in its central meaning: Complete wholeness, having its essential nature within, but being fully expressed without.

Peter, James, and John witnessed the transfiguration of Jesus as an actual event. They could not explain it. Yet the event is consistent with the findings of modern scientists that everything visible can be converted to energy, and that the universe is awash in energy. It also agrees with the experience of many of us in the healing field, who have seen light surrounding people.

We can no longer believe that Moses and Jesus were unique in being enfolded in white light. These were natural phenomena and not supernatural. With the advance of knowledge, however, we have gained more than we have lost. These accounts of Moses' and Jesus' appearance are based on fact. The energetic or etheric body, which provides the formative and sustaining pattern for the physical body, is experienced as *light*. This is what the apostles saw, and it fits closely with the meaning of the Greek term for "transfigured."

James Eden, in his book, *Energetic Healing*, gives corroborating evidence for the reality of the energetic body. Also, Kendall Johnson, who worked with Thelma Moss at UCLA, writes:

115

"Our experiments with radiation field photography and the Kirlian effect have led us to the conclusion that there is in each living organism an energy matrix or template that provides an underlying structure for its material body. The corona or edge effect that we have observed is the telltale evidence of that matrix."**1**

The light, then, has always been present in all of us, though hitherto unknown and unrecognized. Knowing this, some of Jesus' statements take on new meaning. He not only declared, "I am the light of the world," (John 8:12; 9:5), but also, "You are the light of the world." (Matthew 5:14) Both in a literal and figurative sense, he knew how to "let the light shine." In Luke 11:34-36, he declares: "Your eye is the lamp of your body; when your eye is sound,2 your whole body is full of light; but when it is not sound, your body is full of darkness. Therefore, be careful lest the light in you be darkness. If then your whole body is full of light, having no part dark, it will be wholly bright, as when a lamp with its rays give you light."

Affirm:

THE RADIANT LIGHT OF THE CHRIST ILLUMINES MY PATH. I AM INSPIRED AND GUIDED IN ALL MY WAYS.

THE RADIANT LIGHT OF THE CHRIST SHINES THROUGH EVERY CELL OF MY BODY, AND I AM HEALED.

THE RADIANT LIGHT OF THE CHRIST SURROUNDS AND ENFOLDS ME WITH ITS PROTECTING POWER.

Returning to the valley below, Jesus arrived suddenly. Perhaps some of the light still shone visibly from him, for "the crowd, when they saw him, were greatly amazed." (9:15) The nine apostles evidently were embarrassed to have him appear at that time. When he asked them what was going on, they didn't answer him. Instead, *the boy's father* spoke up and explained that the disciples had failed to heal his son.

We leave the work of diagnosis to medical doctors, who are professionally trained in this area. In this case, however, the nature of the condition is obvious. Mark 9:18 lists symptoms of grand mal epilepsy: seizures, falling down, foaming at the mouth, grinding of teeth, and rigidity. People in that time and place held conflicting beliefs about the cause of this condition. Some people, who were into astrology, attributed epilepsy to the adverse influence of the full moon. Others, like the youth's father, believed that it was due to possession by a demon or unclean spirit. Neither of these beliefs is compatible either with contemporary medical theory *or* with modern healing experience.

Despite the records in which this account is preserved, it is difficult to believe that Jesus actually held to either view.3 What is certain is that he attributed the initial failure to heal the young man to a lack of faith.4 This included both the nine apostles who did not go with Jesus to the mountain, and the other people present. That is to say, they lacked the trust and inward certainty of God's presence and power that releases healing. According to the account in Matthew and Luke, he also criticized their lack of mental focus, as they mentally turned in various directions.5 Such mental confusion also gets in the way of healing. So they not only doubted the power of God, but also lacked any central focus in their consciousness.

The New Testament Letter of James is usually thought of as supporting a doctrine of works, but it also gives excellent advice regarding faith:

"If any of you lacks wisdom, let him ask God, who gives to all men generously and without reproaching, and it will be given him. But let him ask in faith, with no doubting, for he who doubts is like a wave of the sea that is driven and tossed by the wind. For that person must not suppose that a double-minded man, unstable in all his ways, will receive anything from the Lord." (1:5-8)

Meditate on the following:

MY ATTENTION IS ON GOD ALONE. THERE IS ONLY ONE PRESENCE AND ONE POWER IN THIS SITUATION, GOD THE GOOD, ALL-GOVERNING.

I LOOK PAST APPEARANCES TO THE GOOD IN EVERY PERSON, EVERY THING, AND EVERY SITUATION.

"THERE IS ONE BODY AND ONE SPIRIT...ONE GOD AND FATHER OF US ALL, WHO IS ABOVE ALL AND THROUGH ALL AND IN ALL." (Ephesians 4:4,6)

Returning to our narrative, we find that Jesus did not simply criticize those who were present. He took the youth's father aside to discuss the background of the case. The father had, of course, become discouraged because of the chronic nature of his son's condition. The disciples' failure to bring healing only made matters worse. He appealed to Jesus: "If you can do anything, have pity on us and help us." (9:22) Note the word *us*. Here is another example of a parent whose anxious doubts, and identification with a child's illness, have become obstacles to healing.

Jesus took the man's phrase, "if you can," and threw it back at him to reconsider. "All things are possible to him who

118

believes." (9:23) The word "possible" in the translation confuses some readers. This does not mean "possible" in the sense of "less than probable." It means that all things can be done or are enabled to those who have the needed faith, trust, and inward expectancy.**6**

The man replied, "I believe; help my unbelief!" (9:24) He thus acknowledged that *he himself needed help*. Although a degree of inner conflict remained, the decisive breakthrough had been made. He had responded positively to Jesus' call for greater trust. "Jesus took him [the man's son] by the hand and lifted him up, and he arose." (9:27)

At first, however, the youth's condition had appeared to worsen. Inwardly, in fact, he was progressing rapidly toward a complete recovery. Several generations of healers have noted that symptoms may temporarily get worse, even while a healing is being completed. This sometimes occurs as harmonious thoughts and images are working strongly to dissolve old, discordant patterns on a subconscious level. This process has been called *chemicalization*, by analogy to what occurs when an acid and an alkali are mixed, such as by adding soda to sour milk.**7**

H. Emilie Cady, a homeopathic physician and author of the basic Unity® text, *Lessons In Truth*, wrote (in 1894):

Should you find yourself at any time in this state of internal excitement with aggravation of old, bad conditions, it needs only that you constantly affirm, "There is nothing to fear, absolutely *nothing* to fear; perfect love reigns, and all is good; peace, be still," etc., and very soon the brighter conditions will appear and you will find yourself on a much higher plane than you have ever been before. Do not be afraid of this word (or the condition) "chemicalization," as many have been, for truly there is nothing to fear in it."**8**

Affirm:

I INVITE   THE ACTION OF DIVINE LOVE TO COMPLETE ITS WORK WITHIN MY SOUL AND BODY. PERFECT LOVE CASTS OUT ALL FEAR.

After the healing was successfully completed, Jesus and his apostles held a private meeting. The nine asked Jesus why they could not heal the youth whose father sought their help. The discussion focused on prayer. There is an obvious point in this: If power seems to wane, do not concentrate on what went wrong. Reviewing a situation in retrospect is useful up to a point. Our main focus, however, should be on continuing the prayer work, and considering what we can do that is useful in the present.

Prayer is not intended here in the sense of begging for something. Jesus wanted his disciples to give their total attention to God, not just to verbally articulate a formula. The word translated "prayer" in Mark 9:29 is *proseuchomai*, from *prosecho*, which means "to pay attention to; to direct the mind." The Greek text, especially with the prefix *pros* (i.e., "toward" or "with reference to"), tells us to focus our attention steadfastly on the Presence of God. The word also implies *communion* (common union) with that to which the mind is directed.

On one extreme, prayer is too technique-oriented, so that the formula itself becomes an obstacle. On the opposite extreme, prayer is haphazard and nebulous, with no specific methods or guidelines. The latter may have been the case here. The apostles sincerely wanted to be effective. They were not fully willing, however, to "pay the price" in terms of mental and spiritual preparation and self-discipline.

Grace is a given, and is free in principle, but it still has to be received and applied in practical ways. We may inherit a hill full of gravel, with a potential profit of a million dollars. Unless we begin working with the needed equipment, however, we won't gain a cent. And, in the life of the Spirit, we do not really receive what is given until we resolutely put aside our mental and spiritual resistance to Its positive, healing action. As Meister Eckhart put it, we let God be God in us. We forgo our own resistance, and this is what affirmative prayer methods help us to do. If we expect to go beyond an occasional healing, and consciously live the larger, freer life that is available, this is still required today.

Declare:

LIGHT AND JOY AND PEACE ABIDE IN ME. MY MIND IS POISED IN PEACE AND BEAUTY. I REST IN CALM TRUST, AND RELY ON THE INDWELLING CHRIST TO BRING GOOD INTO MY EXPERIENCE.

Chapter 16

The Man Born Blind

1As he passed by, he saw a man blind from his birth. 2And his disciples asked him, "Rabbi, who sinned, this man or his parents, that he was born blind?" 3Jesus answered, "It was not that this man sinned, or his parents, but that the works of God might be made manifest in him. 4We must work the works of him who sent me, while it is day; the night comes, when no one can work. 5As long as I am in the world, I am the light of the world." 6As he said this, he spat on the ground and made clay of the spittle and anointed the man's eyes with the clay, 7saying to him, "Go, wash in the pool of Siloam" (which means Sent). So he went and washed and came back seeing. 8The neighbors and those who had seen him before as a beggar, said, "Is not this the man who used to sit and beg?" 9Some said, "It is he"; others said, "No, but he is like him." He said, "I am the man." 10They said to him,"Then how were your eyes opened?" 11He answered, "The man called Jesus made clay and anointed my eyes and said to me, 'Go to Siloam and wash'; so I went and washed and received my sight." 12They said to him, "Where is he?" He said, "I do not know."
–John 9:1-12

The narrative following in John 9:13-34, involving the healed man's interrogation and his parents' evasion, has the feeling of actual dialogue. We reject the dogma, held by some, that the Gospel of John *must* be less historically accurate than the Gospels of Matthew, Mark, and Luke. Yet the designation, by Clement of Alexandria, of John as "The Spiritual Gospel" has a valid point. In its author's paradigm, eternal life is a present reality. Indeed, when we engage the images and the text of John in an active way, we are led inevitably beyond ordinary boundaries of thought. This chapter will serve as an example.

The question, "who sinned, this man or his parents, that he was born blind?" (9:2) implies that Jesus' disciples believed in reincarnation, or at least considered it as a possibility. If a person, blind since birth, was in this condition due to his misconduct, the sin or sins would have had to occur in a previous life, either on the earth plane or in some other realm of existence. The doctrine of karma, taught in Hinduism and Buddhism, maintains that the process of reaping the results of our thoughts and actions, either for good or for ill, carries over beyond a single lifetime. The disciples' question, however, also suggests the possibility that God may have punished the man because of the sins of his parents.

The prophet Ezekiel, one of the architects of post-exilic Judaism (see Ezekiel, Chapter 18), repudiated the view that children are punished for their parents' sins. In a general sense, of course, children are strongly influenced by what their parents say and do, and even by what they think. This is not, however, the claim that Ezekiel rejected. His general conclusion contained a specific historical purpose: to discredit the excuse that the leaders of Judah had been exiled in Babylonia because of their parents' misdeeds, or those of their grandparents or great grandparents. Rather, he recognized that it is something they brought on themselves, for reasons too far-ranging to discuss here.

The strongest argument supporting karma and reincarnation as an explanation for the man's blindness–from birth–is that no one has come forward with a better or more likely idea. The lack of a better idea is not proof. It does suggest, however, that in a universe of moral order, the idea may have merit.

The way that the text is usually translated and punctuated, Jesus appears to have offered a third explanation, "that the works of God might be made manifest in him." In other words, God intervened to make the man blind from birth, so that Jesus could later heal him and thus demonstrate God's power working through him. This is unlikely, for two reasons. *First*, there is serious doubt that the translators have constructed the sentences correctly. The early Greek manuscripts had no punctuation and no spaces between words. Thus, there is often a valid area of judgment as to how and where to punctuate. Merely switching a comma and a period yields a radically different view of Jesus' response:

"It was not that this man sinned, or his parents. But that the works of God might be made manifest in him, we must work the works of him who sent me, while it is day; night comes, when no one can work."

Read in this way, what the text actually affirms is Jesus' felt need to act now, before opposition to him and his activities in Jerusalem became too great. This makes sense because it fits the historical context.

Second, it is totally contrary to the writer's own experience, and that of his colleagues, to think that God plays games in this way. God does not willfully blind people, so that a healer (or God) can act as a metaphysical "show off" at a later date. The Creator and Lord of the universe has no need to prove Himself, and no need to show His authority in this way.

How the man became blind is really beside the point. What needed to be done was to restore the man's sight, not to elaborate on how the condition came about. The disciples' question, moreover, was impertinent and, in modern terms, unprofessional. In effect, they asked him to reveal information about a specific person who was not their concern. This was reason enough for Jesus to cut off the discussion.

The question is not only, "Does reincarnation occur?," but also, "What do we do with the concept after we have accepted it?" If we answer "yes" to the first question, this does not justify making reincarnation the basis of *a spirituality of postponement.* (We have had more than enough of this in the history of Christianity, and it would be a mistake to reintroduce it under a new pretext.) Had Jesus given a discourse on karma and reincarnation at the Pool of Siloam, he may have been technically correct, even intellectually stimulating. He would, however, by the same action have blocked his own effectiveness as a healing channel. That is to say, the man would have remained as blind as the day he was born.

Jesus acted in the realization that God is omnipresent *now*, All-in-all. This is not a mere hope or a future expectation, for the truth is that we are *now* one with God. Our true position in the Mind of God is not only as an expression of the Divine Word–we are, in reality, the Divine Word *being* expressed. Knowing this as an actual experience, we are lifted consciously into a karma-less state of being. We can all choose–in actual fact, we *must* choose–between a spirituality of karma, retribution and guilt on the one hand, and a spirituality of freedom, grace, and forgiveness on the other hand. Jesus, in this text, emphasizes that God's healing power is available now, and now is the time to attune ourselves with the Divine Omnipresence.

This leads to another key question: Is every condition one that we should seek to heal? According to this text, the answer is clearly *yes*. As Paul affirmed, "Behold, now is the acceptable time; now is the day of salvation." (II Corinthians 6:2) The greatest teachers in our field have held this view. Emmet Fox declared, "Christ is Lord of karma." Malinda E. Cramer emphasized, "We do not work *toward* Principle. We work *from* Principle."

Deep-seated karmic conditions can be healed, and sometimes are. Even when physical healing does not occur, however, there is no real failure. The prayer work nevertheless strengthens people on the path of spiritual wholeness, and helps them to meet their needs on a deep level. We find this in countless people who have achieved great things in spite of physical limitations. The Hospice Movement, also, has taught us that healing can take more than one form, and that so-called death can be a forward step in the soul's progress.

What is most significant in this account is Jesus' use of an I AM statement. The traditional interpretation of the I AM statements in the Gospel of John is that they are theological claims about Jesus as a personality, and him only. Quite the contrary, they are a method that *anyone* can use to identify with God.

Let us consider how Jesus worked. Before restoring the man's sight, he declared, "I am the light of the world." (John 8:12; 9:5) *He thus identified with the divine quality which is the opposite of blindness, whether the lack of sight be spiritual or physical, or both.* Before raising Lazarus from the dead, he identified with the divine idea of life: "I am the resurrection and the life." (John 11:25) In connection with multiplying the loaves and fishes, he identified with the divine reality of God as universal supply: "I am the bread of life." (John 6:35,48)

I AM statements work to the extent that they free us from false identifications, and lead us to a consciousness of our eternal nature as God's Idea, I AM, The Word, or The Christ. In the I AM statement, there is an implied predicate, the verb "to be." Thus, "I am the light of the world" means, in effect, "I AM *is* the light of the world." Interestingly enough, Jesus made the same claim for everyone: "*You* are the light of the world." (Matthew 5:14)

Jesus did not invent the I AM statement. Nor, as some scholars believe, have the I AM statements been mistakenly attributed to him. The noncanonical Gospel of Thomas includes I AM statements, and even the Gospel of Mark has one.1 So the evidence for them is not limited only to the Gospel of John.

According to an ancient tradition, Jesus returned to Egypt as a young man, in order to continue his education. If he did so, he would have encountered the use of I AM statements there. Many Egyptians used such statements as a way of identifying with Isis, the Egyptian goddess of motherhood and fertility. The practice also spread far beyond Egypt as a kind of magical formula, in which people identified with various gods, goddesses, angels, and even demons.2

Jesus' innovation was to use this method to identify with the Allness of God, as one unified Presence and Power. He took spiritual consciousness to its final step within the context of Allness. At the same time, he rejected the practice of identifying with fictitious gods, goddesses, angels, and demons in an attempt to achieve limited goals. For example, Thomas #77 reads: "It is I who am the all. From me did the all come forth, and unto me did the all extend." In this way, Jesus ventured beyond the magic and superstition with which I AM statements were widely associated at the time. Instead, he worked out the larger implications of God's central revelation to Moses as recorded in

128

Exodus 3:14-15:

> God said to Moses, "I AM WHO I AM." And he said, "Say this to the people of Israel, 'I AM has sent me to you.'...this is my name forever, and thus I am to be remembered throughout all generations."

Most people would be reluctant to identify with God in this way, as Jesus did. Yet using I AM statements, in helping us to identify with our Divine Parent, also helps us to awaken to the vital core of our being, which is one with God. In the same action, we discover that although we retain our individuality, we are also one with all people everywhere. We are not only one *with* God; we are also one *in* God. This is the great insight underlying Paul's statement: "There is neither Jew nor Greek, there is neither slave nor free, there is neither male nor female; for you are all one in Christ Jesus." (Galatians 3:28) In this consciousness, we really do transcend all boundaries of race, religion, age, gender, and national origin. Of course, it is impossible to use I AM statements effectively as an expression of egotism or superiority over others.

Also in this account, Jesus followed his usual practice of persuading the one needing help to take a positive step, as an expression of trust: "Go, wash in the pool of Siloam....So he went and washed and came back seeing." (9:7) This tells us that the I AM statement is not enough in itself. It requires follow-up thinking and action, in line with the discovery of our spiritual Identity.

On a symbolic level, washing the clay from his eyes points to our own need to wash away the clay of material beliefs and limitations. When the clay is removed from our inner vision, we see, and therefore experience, life as we never have before. We discover, to our wonder and amazement, that God's wisdom and harmony rule the cosmos and all its parts. In this realization, karma is superseded by grace, and healings that would otherwise be impossible, actually occur.

Chapter 17

Three Additional Accounts

Three healing accounts in the Gospel of Luke are too sparse in their information to justify separate chapters. Yet they are part of the total record and valuable for that reason.

14Now he was casting out a demon that was dumb; when the demon had gone out, the dumb man spoke, and the people marveled. 15"But some of them said, "He casts out demons by Beelzebul, the prince of demons."; 16while others, to test him, sought from him a sign from heaven. 17But he, knowing their thoughts, said to them, "Every kingdom divided against itself is laid waste, and house falls upon house. 18And if Satan also is divided against himself, how will his kingdom stand? For you say that I cast out demons by Beelzebul. 19And if I cast out demons by Beelzebul, by whom do your sons cast them out? Therefore, they shall be your judges. 20But it if is by the finger of God that I cast out demons, then the kingdom of God has come upon you. 21When a strong man, fully armed, guards his own palace, his goods are in peace; 22but when one stronger than he assails him and overcomes him, he takes away his armor in which he trusted, and divides his spoil. 23He who is not with me is against me, and he who does not gather with me scatters."
–Luke 11:14-23 (parallel passages: Matthew 9:32-34; 12:22-30)

The record gives us the bare facts that the man could not talk, but that Jesus restored his ability to speak. The way that this material is organized in Luke shows signs of editing, and is not historically reliable in the form in which we find it. Nevertheless, we can be confident on two points. *First,* such healings were often interpreted as exorcisms, in which demons or unclean spirits were cast out. *Second,* some of Jesus' critics had the audacity to claim that he cast out demons by the prince of demons. Thus, they equated God's healing action with a form of Satanism.

Apparently Beelzebul (also called Baal-Zebub and Beelzebub) began as a Canaanite deity. The name means "lord of filth" or "lord of the flies." By the time of Jesus, the Baal religion had long ceased to function in Palestine. In this respect, the prophets of Israel had been successful. Beelzebul continued in the popular imagination, however, in a demoted form. He had become a boss demon with lesser demons working under him.

Elizabeth B. Howes shows deep insight when she writes:

Judging by his [Jesus'] evaluation that this was blasphemy, the one sin "that hath not forgiveness," it must be concluded that he saw their accusation as a deliberate perversion of truth. They had stood in his presence, had heard what he had been saying, and had seen what was happening, but to defend their own rigidities, they called his activities "of the devil." It is not, then, that they failed to see his truth, not that they ran from it, but rather that seeing it they mislabeled it. To deny the value or to turn one's back on it is a totally different psychological and moral act from facing it and calling it evil. To do this is a perversion of moral discrimination. Pharisees and Jesus would have known the passage from Isaiah, "Woe unto them that call evil good and good evil."**1**

One of the striking images in this passage is *the finger of God.* Jesus declares: "If it is by the finger of God that I cast out demons, then the kingdom of God has come upon you." (11:20)

This affirms in effect that healing from the inside out, the mending of creation, is a sign of the will and rule of God. The metaphor, "finger of God," is from ancient Babylonia. Archaeologists have found a seven-foot high pillar, carved in stone in the form of a gigantic finger, which depicts the Babylonian sun-god Shamash. He is shown near its top, handing King Hammurabi (1792-1750 B.C.) a scroll of 250 laws, which are inscribed below in the stone. It thus pictures a deity as the source of law, a code which is delegated to a human king to honor and enforce.

Old Testament scholars have documented the influence of Babylonian law on the Israelites. According to the Book of Exodus, when Moses outdid the Pharaoh's magicians in Egypt, they acknowledged, "This is the finger of God." (Exodus 8:19) In Exodus 31:18, we read, "And he gave to Moses, when he had made an end of speaking with him upon Mount Sinai, the two tables of the testimony, tables of stone, written with the finger of God."

The "tables of the testimony" were the Ten Commandments. They were the Israelites' charter of freedom, spiritually and politically. They proclaimed that God is One, and forbade idolatry. Equally important, they provided the moral framework by which they could function as a free people. Reflecting a realm of universal law, they require, for example, that human life and property be respected, and that husbands and wives, parents and children, have mutual rights and obligations. *In a slave culture, none of these standards count for anything.* Under their guidance, the Israelites completed the movement that Moses began. Once a nation of slaves, they became a free people with an undying passion for liberty. The metaphor of the finger of God thus expanded its meaning to include freedom as well as law.

Thus, in declaring that he casts out demons (however defined) by the finger of God, Jesus points to a new exodus of the soul. In his vision, not just given individuals, but humanity as a whole, will move symbolically out of Egyptian bondage and into the Promised Land. We gain liberty within God's realm of universal law. *This has nothing to do with geography.* It means deliverance out of error and spiritual darkness, and into a new realization of health, wisdom, love, abundance, and peace.

What is more, to the degree that the individual is attuned to the Indwelling Christ, he or she enjoys living in eternity now. For in truth, we are already in the Kingdom of God and can enjoy its benefits, here and now. The healings of Jesus, in addition to meeting the immediate needs of given persons, were signs pointing to *universal* healing and illumination, and were intended as such.

If people will take this seriously and recognize the connection (real as well as etymological) between holiness and wholeness, they can be relieved of a variety of false attitudes. Some mystics have claimed, in error, that the body is the prison house of the soul. As Jesus makes clear in his healing ministry, the challenge is the reverse: The soul has become the prison house of the body. The soul holds the keys to the cell block, and only the soul can relinquish them. The good news, of course, is that it need not be that way. When the negativity and discord in the soul are healed by an influx of spiritual consciousness, the body is healed as a result of this inner renewal.

God's vision sees us whole and harmonious both in soul and in body. In the markets of the Near East, merchants often use the expression, "finger of God," to praise their products. Being grounded in biblical imagery, this practice probably dates back to biblical times, differing only in the word used for God. Rocco Errico states:

To make an impression, the seller will say, "In the most precious name of Allah, this rug was done by His hand," or "the finger of Allah made this garment." What the merchant means is "the rug is perfect" and "the garment is flawless." To have the hand or finger of God involved in anything is a beautiful way of saying, "This is the finest craftsmanship in the world." The rug, garment, or other merchandise is equated with God to show absolute perfection, ultimate beauty, and excellence.[2]

Affirm:

THE KINGDOM OF GOD IS WITHIN ME NOW.

I DECLARE THE ALL-SUFFICIENT POWER OF GOD TO BE THE ONLY POWER IN MY MIND, BODY, AND AFFAIRS.

I FEAR NOT, FOR IT IS THE FATHER'S GOOD PLEASURE TO GIVE ME THE KINGDOM OF LIFE, LIGHT, AND LOVE.

I TURN TO GOD IN PRAYER, KNOWING THAT I AM AN HEIR OF GOD TO ALL GOOD, AND A JOINT HEIR WITH JESUS THE CHRIST.

I LET GO OF OLD HABIT PATTERNS THAT HAVE BOUND ME. I JOYOUSLY ACCEPT MY FREEDOM IN CHRIST.

I LIVE, MOVE, AND HAVE MY BEING IN THE NEWNESS OF THE HEALING CHRIST.

I WORK WITH THE CREATIVE SPIRIT OF GOD TO FULFILL MY PART IN THE DIVINE PLAN.

AS A FREE CHILD OF GOD, I LET FORGIVENESS AND
JOY FLOW THROUGH ME AS A CLEANSING, FREEING
CURRENT OF LIFE TO ALL PEOPLE EVERYWHERE.

**10Now he was teaching in one of the synagogues on the
Sabbath. 11And there was a woman who had had a [spirit of]
infirmity for eighteen years; she was bent over and could not
fully straighten herself. 12And when Jesus saw her, he called
her and said to her, "Woman, you are freed from your
infirmity." 13And he laid his hands upon her, and
immediately she was made straight, and she praised God.
14But the ruler of the synagogue, indignant because Jesus
had healed on the sabbath, said to the people, "There are six
days on which work ought to be done; come on those days
and be healed, and not on the sabbath day." 15Then the
Lord answered him, "You hypocrites! Does not each of you
on the sabbath untie his ox or his ass from the manger, and
lead it away to water it? 16And ought not this woman, a
daughter of Abraham, [whom Satan] bound for eighteen
years, be loosed from this bond on the sabbath day?" 17As
he said this, all his adversaries were put to shame; and all the
people rejoiced at all the glorious things that were done by
him.**
–Luke 13:10-17

In its present form, this account is self-contradictory on its
face. That is to say, it pictures Jesus using affirmative prayer,
whereas the patient is claimed to be possessed by "a spirit of
infirmity."

In comparing the healing records in Mark and Luke, we find
that the author of Luke has a strong editorial bias toward demon
possession. It is likely that he modified his source, adding "spirit

of" in 13:11 and "whom Satan" in 13:16. A bent back does not indicate possession by an outside entity. Also, claiming that the woman was possessed does not fit Jesus' statement, "Woman, *you are freed* from your infirmity." (13:12) He affirmed that it is so; he did not say, "come out," or even "be freed." He meant that the woman was already one with God and therefore, in truth, whole and free.

In addition, certain patterns are repeated. Again, Jesus heals on the Sabbath, keeping the spiritual Sabbath of inner peace while ignoring the letter of the law. He again touches the patient. Further, he exposes the absurdity of opposing arguments. Like a Greek rhetorician, he argues from the lesser to the greater. How foolish it is to lead one's ox or ass to water (viewed as acceptable by the ruler of the synagogue, and the Pharisees in general, on the Sabbath), while at the same time keeping one of God's children in misery.

The main difference is that here he does not wait for the person to seek him out. He takes the initiative by calling her and declaring her wholeness to be a present fact. This was certainly justified. Jesus had agreed to present the day's lesson in the synagogue, and the woman had come to the meeting with a serious spiritual purpose (whether or not this included a healing purpose).

Of course, it is always right to hold positive thoughts and images toward others, whether or not we call these good thoughts "prayers." There are only two other choices, both of which are insulting: to visualize evil and discord, or to try to hold our minds a blank. Those who think otherwise, interestingly enough, have never developed a serious methodology for holding their own minds a blank.

What we do *not* do is try to mentally bind or limit others to a given course of action. This is mental malpractice, and is strongly discouraged by responsible practitioners of New Thought. It is safe, rather, to turn others over to God in our consciousness, affirming Divine Order and right action. Then God's universal good prevails, instead of our limited view of the good.

If you want to improve the general betterment of humanity, affirm:

I BEHOLD ALL PEOPLE, EVERYWHERE, IN THE PURE WHITE LIGHT OF THE CHRIST.

A good affirmation for world peace is:

LET LIBERTY, JUSTICE, PEACE, LOVE, AND UNDERSTANDING BE ESTABLISHED IN ME AND THROUGHOUT THE EARTH, IN THE NAME OF JESUS CHRIST.

For all political leaders, declare:

THROUGH THE CHRIST MIND, YOU ARE UNIFIED IN THOUGHT, PURPOSE, AND UNDERSTANDING, AND INSPIRED TO RIGHT ACTION FOR THE SECURITY AND FREEDOM OF ALL MANKIND.

1One Sabbath when he went to dine at the house of a ruler who belonged to the Pharisees, they were watching him. 2And behold, there was a man before him who had dropsy. 3And Jesus spoke to the lawyers and Pharisees, saying, "Is it lawful to heal on the Sabbath, or not?" 4But they were silent. Then he took him and healed him, and let him go. 5And he

said to them, "Which of you, having an ass or an ox that has fallen into a well, will not immediately pull him out on a Sabbath day?" 6And they could not reply to this.
--Luke 14:1-6

From this record, it is likely that the Pharisee who hosted the Sabbath dinner intentionally invited a sick man into the house, to see whether Jesus would heal him on the Sabbath. Of course, he did so, with the realization that the Divine Presence is here and available seven days a week. Also, Jesus again confuted the Pharisees on their own ground. Even their rigid rules allowed them to rescue a domestic animal from a well on the Sabbath.

The account implies that when our wills are united with God's will, healing is simple and natural. It is released through the peace of God, which is what the Sabbath is really about. Jesus, by healing on the Sabbath as often as he did, evidently intended to make a statement–or, to put it more precisely, to perform a parable of action–to that effect. Making whole is accomplished in the realization that God's work is already complete.

Chapter 18

Bartimaeus's Sight Restored

46And they came to Jericho; and as he was leaving Jericho with his disciples and a great multitude, Bartimaeus, a blind beggar, the son of Timaeus, was sitting by the roadside. 47And when he heard that it was Jesus of Nazareth, he began to cry out and say, "Jesus, Son of David, have mercy on me!" 48And many rebuked him, telling him to be silent; but he cried out all the more, "Son of David, have mercy on me!" 49And Jesus stopped and said, "Call him." And they called the blind man, saying to him, "Take heart; rise, he is calling you." 50And throwing off his mantle, he sprang up and came to Jesus. 51And Jesus said to him, "What do you want me to do for you?" And the blind man said to him, "Master, let me receive my sight." 52And Jesus said to him, "Go your way; your faith has made you well." And immediately he received his sight and followed him on the way.
–Mark 10:46-52 (parallel passages: Matthew 20:29-34; Luke 18:35-43)

The story of Bartimaeus is based on an actual healing, but it is also a beautifully written parable. It represents the soul being reunited with its Divine Source, the Indwelling God. It tells us that healing is more than an occasional recovery of mental or physical well-being. Wholeness in the larger sense involves a changed belief structure and a new image of self. The account carries the implicit understanding that whatever we conceive reality to be–including our own reality–is reflected back to us like a mirror.

141

Bartimaeus is from *bar* (son of), and *Timaeus* (contaminated, defiled, unclean, impure). The name is likely to be allegorical rather than actual, for it signifies a defiled state of thought and belief, leading to the conditions referred to in the text. As the scene opens, Bartimaeus, a blind beggar, sits by the side of the road. He has three limitations:

(1) *Blind*–physically sightless, and also ignorant of spiritual truth, including his true status as a son of God.

(2) *A beggar*–begging for his daily bread, and also possessed by a belief in lack.

(3) *Sitting by the roadside*–not really living, but only existing; a spectator, but not a participant in life, unaware of his spiritual heritage.

Jesus and his disciples are passing through Jericho on the way to Jerusalem. They are part of a great crowd of people. This is plausible historically, since large numbers of Galileans took this route to Jerusalem each year to celebrate Passover. It was the route to travel from Galilee to Jerusalem without going through Samaria, which they deliberately avoided.

The original Passover led to the release of the Israelites from Egyptian bondage, and sent them on their way to the Promised Land. The trip's implied meaning, then, is to pass from a condition of slavery, sorrow, and lack into a consciousness of freedom, joy, and plenty. Jerusalem, the crowd's destination, means "habitation of peace."

When Bartimaeus heard that Jesus was near, he cried out repeatedly, "Jesus, son of David, have mercy on me!" (10:47) This is like the estranged soul when it cries out emotionally to its inner Source, its inner Messiah, the Christ. The crowd's rebuke tells us that the soul's spiritual rebirth will be resisted by the false beliefs and images that were once dominant within us. The transition from spiritual death to spiritual rebirth and new life in

142

Christ is seldom easy. Bartimaeus continued to cry out to Jesus until he had a response. The message here is to keep on declaring the Word to ourselves until true insight dawns.

Bartimaeus's cries were not in vain. Jesus stopped and told his companions to call him. The crowd that had resisted him changed their attitude and became favorable. "They called the blind man, saying to him, 'Take heart; rise, he is calling you.'" (10:49) It is significant that the Greek word *egeiro*, translated "rise," means not only to rise physically, but also to wake up. His spiritual awakening had begun.

After a sustained program of affirmation and visualization, such a change will occur in your emotional nature. Subconscious energies which formerly resisted your progress will now flow in a positive direction, according to your highest aspirations. Love and trust will replace hate and fear. As blocks to expanded awareness are removed, the expanded vision of Christ Consciousness replaces negative images of sickness and scarcity.

The account repeats the pattern of three. In answering Jesus' call, Bartimaeus (1) *threw off his mantle*, (2) *sprang up*, and (3) *came to Jesus*. The mantle mentioned here, called a *himation*, was a large outer garment. Men who used one wore it during the day, and sometimes slept in it at night. In this context, it represents throwing off a covering of mental misperceptions and emotional defenses. He no longer tried to wrap errors and illusions around his mind, or to sleep in them. He was ready to be made whole, to enter into a new way of being as well as of doing, and he took positive steps in that direction.

Springing to his feet means that he arose spiritually, taking a stand in his larger capacities of mind and spirit.

When he approached Jesus, he depended on his *ears* for direction, being yet blind. This means that he was *open and receptive* to the Indwelling Christ, which was both his core Identity and his inner Teacher.

Being asked to state his request, Bartimaeus replied: "'Master, let me receive my sight.' And Jesus said to him, 'Go your way; your faith has made you well.'" (10:51-52) Again, the emphasis is on applied faith as the way to healing. Also, the word translated "well" is *sozo*, as in Chapter 9. It means to restore both inwardly and outwardly, in soul and in body.

"And immediately he received his sight and followed him on the way." (10:52) Thus, he not only received his sight, but without hesitation went with Jesus to Jerusalem to celebrate the feast of Passover. This represents a transition that is open to all, in symbolic terms, out of Egyptian bondage and into the Promised Land. Its goal is Jerusalem, a consciousness of inner peace. You, too, can leave behind false limitations, and enter into the freedom and fullness of the life of Christ.

Let us then know, not merely hope or believe, that the Healing Christ *is* our life. "When Christ, who is our life, is manifested, then you too will be manifested with him in glory." (Colossians 3:4, New English Bible) The promise of Jesus' teachings, his healings, and his own resurrection is that universal harmony shall become manifest through all and as all. This reality is even now unfolding from the inside out, as in Jesus' image of an unfolding lily that exceeds Solomon in all his glory. In the words of the Lord's Prayer, stated in the affirmative as in the original Aramaic: "Thy kingdom has come, thy will is done, as in heaven, so on Earth."

Notes

Introduction

1. Eden, James; *Energetic Healing: The Merging of Ancient and Modern Medical Practices*; New York, Plenum Press, c. 1993, p. 222

2. Fox, Emmet; *The Sermon on the Mount*; New York, Harper & Brothers, c. 1934, 1935, 1938, p. 53

3. Errico, Rocco; *The Message of Matthew*; Irvine, CA., Noohra Foundation, 1991, p. 21, n. 13

Chapter 1

1. Lamsa, George; *More Light on the Gospel*; Garden City, NY, Doubleday, c. 1968, p. 58

2. The Gospel of John, unlike Mark–and Matthew and Luke, which draw from the Marcan tradition extensively–*never pictures Jesus as an exorcist.* In this respect, the Gospel of John may well be *more* historically accurate than Matthew, Mark, and Luke.

Chapter 2

1. In the Greek text, *puretos* means "a fever" and *puresso* is "to suffer from a fever." The Greek noun for fire, *pur*, has the same Indo-European root as the English terms *pure, purify*, and *pyre*.

2. See two books by Dolores Krieger, *The Therapeutic Touch*, published by Prentice-Hall; and *Accepting Your Power to Heal*, published by Bear & Company.

3. Jung, Carl G.; *Man and His Symbols*; Garden City, NY., Prentice-Hall, c. 1964, p. 58

Chapter 3

1. Throckmorton, Burton H. Jr., Editor; *Gospel Parallels: A Synopsis of the First Three Gospels*; New York, Thomas Nelson & Sons, c. 1949, 1957, p. 32

Chapter 4

1. Charlesworth, James H., Editor; *The Old Testament Pseudepigrapha, Volume I, Apocalyptic Literature and Testaments*; Garden City, NY., Doubleday, c. 1983, pp. 785-786

Chapter 6

1. *Gospel Parallels*; op cit, p. 51

2. Cramer, Malinda E.; *Harmony*, Vol. 6, No. 9, June 1894, p. 278. The New Testament Letter to the Hebrews, Chapters 3 and 4, discusses the Sabbath consciousness of rest.

Chapter 7

1. Again, the word translated "authority" is *exousia*, "out of being or substance." Using a form of the verb "to be," it alludes to the I AM, to being in Its absolute and unconditioned state.

2. Quoted by C. K. Barrett in his book, *The Gospel According to St. John*; London, SPCK, c. 1962, p. 208

Chapter 9

1. The Greek word translated "well" or "whole" is *sozo*, a strong term which means "to save from spiritual and physical death." *Sozo* is here in the perfect tense [*sesoken*], signifying permanency. This certainly supports "whole" as the preferred translation.

2. Jesus did not tell her merely to "go in peace," but to "enter into [*eis*, not *en*] peace." That is to say, enter into a condition of peace. The verb *hygies*, a cognate of the English word *hygiene*, translated "healed," is present imperative and implies continuous action. He meant: "Be continually whole."

Chapter 11

1. Again, the word translated "believe" is *pisteuo*, with the emphasis not on blind belief, but on inner assurance, confidence, and trust.
    The Aramaic tradition of the text essentially agrees. Commenting on the word translated "believe" in Matthew 9:28, Rocco Errico points out that it is "Mhaymneen from Mhaymnah and means *to believe, have faith, have confidence in, to be faithful, trusted*. It comes from the Aramaic root word Amen meaning *to make firm, to be constant, persevere, persist, steadfast*." (*The Message of Matthew*, op cit., p. 36, n. 24) Emphasis is in the original.

2. *The Journal of Religion and Psychical Research*, Vol. 17, No. 2, April 1994, article on "Role Theory and Exceptional Human Experiences" by Rhea White, p, 76

1. Johnson, Kendall; *The Living Aura: Radiation Field Photography and the Kirlian Effect*; New York, Hawthorn Books, c. 1975, p. 120

2. The adjective translated "sound" (or "single" in the King James Version) in Luke 11:34 and Matthew 6:22-23 is *haplous*. It is from the Greek verb *pleko*, which means "to weave together as a pattern." Seeing things single in the Omnipresence of God means seeing everything as patterned and interconnected, the oneness of the universal and the individual. The metaphor of the seamless garment in John 19:23 has essentially the same meaning.

3. Commenting on the term found in Matthew's version, specifically 17:18, Rocco Errico states: "In Aramaic the noun Sheda *lunatic, demon* is used to describe an unhealthy physical or psychological mood, state or condition." (*The Message of Matthew*, op cit., p. 70, n. 13)

4. "Faithless" translates *apistos*, which consists of *a-* (the alpha privative, meaning "the exact opposite of"), and *pistis* (the word for faith, trust, inward certainty).

5. Matthew 17:17 and Luke 9:41 include the term *diestrammene*, translated "perverse." The Greek word, however, actually means "turning in various directions" mentally and emotionally, and does not imply that the people present were morally perverted.

6. "All things are possible to him who believes" translates the sentence, *panta dunata to pisteuonti*. *Dunata*, translated "possible," has no trace of doubt or improbability. It is a form of *dunatos*, which means "powerful, capable, able." It is derived from the verb *dunamai*, "I am able, I can, I am of power, I have the power." We also need to remember that

pisteuo means more than mere belief. It is a state of inner assurance, agreement, yielding, and trust.

7. Three references from the late 1800s show that chemicalization is not a recent discovery, but has been known and recognized since the early days of New Thought. This is apparent in *Class Lessons 1888* by Emma Curtis Hopkins, compiled and edited by Elizabeth C. Bogart, Marina del Rey, CA., DeVorss, c. 1977, pp. 236-240; *Harmony*, Vol. 2, No. 8, May 1890, pp. 228-229; and *Lessons in Truth* by H. Emilie Cady, Kansas City, Unity Tract Society, undated but first published in 1894, pp. 68-70 (found in early editions only).

8. *Lessons in Truth*; Ibid, p. 70. Emphasis is in the original.

Chapter 16

1. Mark 6:50 has Jesus affirm, "Take heart, it is I; have no fear." "It is I," however, mistranslates *ego eimi*, which actually means "I am."

2. Meyer, Marvin W., Editor; *The Ancient Mysteries: A Sourcebook*; San Francisco, Harper & Row, c. 1987, pp. 172-176

Chapter 17

1. Howes, Elizabeth B.; *Jesus' Answer to God*; San Francisco, Guild for Psychological Studies Publishing House, c. 1984, p. 72. The Bible quotation is from Isaiah 5:20.

2. Errico, Rocco; *Let There Be Light: The Seven Keys*; Marina del Rey, CA., DeVorss, c. 1985, pp. 19-20

Scriptural Index of Healing Accounts in the Gospels

The man with an unclean spirit–Mark 1:21-28 (Luke 4:31-37)

Peter's mother-in-law–Mark 1:29-31 (Matthew 8:14-15; Luke 4:38-39)

A leper cleansed–Mark 1:40-45 (Matthew 8:1-4; Luke 5:12-16)

Ten lepers cleansed–Luke 17:11-19

Paralytic carried by four men–Mark 2:1-12 (Matthew 9:1-8; Luke 5:17-26)

Sick man at pool of Bethzatha–John 5:2-14ff

The man with a withered hand–Luke 6:6-11; Matthew 12:9-14; Mark 3:1-6)

The centurion's servant–Luke 7:2-10 (Matthew 8:5-13)

The official's son–John 4:46-54

The swine miracle–Mark 5:1-20 (Matthew 8:28-34; Luke 8:26-39)

The woman with an issue of blood–Mark 5:25-34 (Matthew 9:20-22; Luke 8:43-48)

Raising of Jairus's daughter–Mark 5:21-24, 35-43 (Matthew 9:18-19, 23-26; Luke 8:40-42, 49-56)

Two blind men indoors–Matthew 9:27-31

The Syrophoenician woman's daughter–Mark 7:24-30 (Matthew 15:21-28)

Deaf man with speech impediment–Mark 7:31-37

Blind man at Bethsaida–Mark 8:22-26

The epileptic boy–Mark 9:14-29 (Matthew 17:14-21; Luke 9:37-43)

The man born blind–John 9:1-12ff

Exorcism of dumb man–Luke 11:14-23 (Matthew 9:32-34; 12:22-30)

The woman bent over–Luke 13:10-17

The man with dropsy–Luke 14:1-6

Bartimaeus's sight restored–Mark 10:46-52 (Matthew 20:29-34; Luke 18:35-43)

Robert Winterhalter graduated from Lakeland College, Sheboygan, Wisconsin (BA), The Iliff School of Theology, Denver, Colorado (MRE), Kentucky Christian University, Ashland, Kentucky (PHD), Unity Training School, Unity Village, Missouri, and Brooks Divinity School, Denver, Colorado.

Robert lived his life through Christ. In his pastoral experience he was minister at the New Thought Temple of Christ, Cleveland, Ohio, minister at the First Divine Science Church, Appleton, Wisconsin, minister at the Universal Center of Truth, Lake County, Illinois, Director of Christ Tower of Prayer, Atlanta, Georgia, minister at the First Divine Science Church, Belleville, Illinois, and Minister of Education Gateway Church of Divine Science, Crestwood, Missouri.

Robert's teaching experience included Teacher Training Coordinator at Unity on the North Shore, Evanston, Illinois, faculty in the Ministerial Education Program at the Christ Church of Truth, Atlanta, Georgia, faculty at the Divine School of Higher Consciousness, Crestwood, Missouri, faculty in the External Degree Program, Hopkins College & Theological Seminary, Clearwater, Florida, and faculty at Divine Science School, Washington, DC.

Robert also served in administrative positions as Chairman of the Board at the Christ Center of Truth, Atlanta, Georgia, as Vice-President of Unity Church on the North Shore, Evanston, Illinois, as Vice-President of the Divine Science Ministers Association Board, as a member of the Academy & Religion & Psychical Research, as Director of District Presidents & Ambassadors-at-large of the International New Thought Alliance, as President of the Society for the Study of Metaphysical Religion (1993-2005), as President of the Greater St. Louis Alliance of New Thought Ministries, and as a board member in the Divine Science Federation International Board of Officers, representing the Divine Science Ministers Association.

Robert was a published author of religious books and articles. This is his fourth book. Previous books include *The Odes of Solomon* (Llewellyn), *The Fifth Gospel* (Harper & Row), and *Jesus' Parables: Finding Our God Within* (Paulist Press).Robert also wrote five curricular courses for Divine Science School, papers and book reviews for the Journal of the Academy of Religion & Psychical Research and the SSMR Journal, and articles in New Thought, Aspire, Dialogue & Distinction, and Wings of Truth.

Robert made his transition from this dimension on March 3, 2010 while this book was being printed.

Other Books Published
by
Ozark Mountain Publishing, Inc.

Continue for more books by Ozark Mountain Publishing, Inc.

Children of the Stars .... by Nikki Pattillo
Angels - The Guardians of Your Destiny ....by Maiya & Geoff Gray-Cobb
Seeds of the Soul...by Maiya Gray-Cobb
The Despiritualized Church...by Rev. Keith Bender
The Science of Knowledge ....by Vara Humphreys
The Other Side of Suicide ....by Karen Peebles
Journey Through Fear ....by Antoinette Lee Howard
Awakening To Your Creation ....by Julia Hanson
Thirty Miracles in Thirty Days ....by Irene Lucas
Windows of Opportunity ....by Sherri Cortland
Why? ....by Mandeep Khera

For more information about any of the above titles, soon to be released titles, or
other items in our catalog, write or visit our website:

OZARK
MOUNTAIN
PUBLISHING
PO Box 754
Huntsville, AR 72740
www.ozarkmt.com
1-800-935-0045/479-738-2348
Wholesale Inquiries Welcome